Key Stage 2 Maths

WORKBOOK 5

Numerical Reasoning Technique

Dr Stephen C Curran
with Katrina MacKay

Edited by Andrea Richardson

This book belongs to

Accelerated Education Publications Ltd

Contents

9. Money & Costs   Pages

1. Units of Currency   3
2. Pounds & Pence   4-9
3. Notes & Coinage   10-16
4. Money Calculations   16-24
5. Fractional Costs   25
6. Money in Words   26-27
7. Problem Solving   27-28

10. Measurement

1. Metric Measurements   29-35
2. Metric Conversions   35-37
3. Decimal Measurements   38-39
4. Reading Metric Scales   40-47
5. Greater Than or Smaller Than   48
6. Rounding Measurements   49
7. Metric Calculations   50-51
8. Imperial Measures   51-52
9. Metric-Imperial Conversions   53
10. Estimating Measurements 54-56
11. Temperature   56-59
12. Problem Solving   59-60

11. Averages

1. Mode   61-62
2. Median   62-63
3. Range   63-64
4. The 'Mean' or Average   64-66
5. Problem Solving   66

Chapter Nine
MONEY & COSTS
1. Units of Currency

Currency is a system of money. Most currencies in the world are based on the Tens Number System (units of ten).

- Most countries in the European Union use the euro (€) and cent as a **Unit of Currency**. There are **one hundred cents** in **one euro**.

- The USA uses dollars ($) and cents. There are **one hundred cents** in **one dollar**.

The United Kingdom uses pounds and pence.

Pounds are written as **£**.   **Pence** are written as **p**.

£1 coin   **1p coin**

There are **one hundred pence** in **one pound**.

$$100p = £1$$

The pound sign (**£**) is written before the number of pounds. The pence sign (**p**) is written after the number of pence. The signs are never used at the same time.

A decimal point is used to separate the pounds (whole ones) from the pence (less than a whole one).

For example, **£4.92** is **4 pounds and 92 pence**.

2. Pounds & Pence

As there are **100 pence** in **one pound**, each penny is worth **one-hundredth** of a pound. This means when pounds and pence are written together using the **£** sign, the pence will only ever be two decimal places. For example:

180p can be written as **£1.80**
23p can be written as **£0.23**
7p can be written as **£0.07**

a. Changing Pounds to Pence

Example: Write **£6.91** as pence.

Step 1 - To change pounds to pence, multiply by **100**. Move the decimal point two places to the right.

$$6.91 \times 100 = 691.0 = 691$$

Step 2 - Change the symbol from **£** to **p**.

Answer: **691p**

Exercise 9: 1   Write the amount as pence:

1) £9.10 = _____
2) £71.05 = _____
3) £195.06 = _____
4) £10.58 = _____
5) £4.23 = _____
6) £2.50 = _____
7) £58.71 = _____
8) £136.94 = _____
9) £3.19 = _____
10) £7.42 = _____

b. Changing Pence to Pounds

Example: Write **903p** as pounds.

Step 1 - To change pence to pounds, divide by **100**. Move the decimal point two places to the left. Remember, a whole number can have a decimal point, so **903** can be written as **903.0**.

$$903.0 \div 100 = 9.03 = 9.03$$

(2 places left)

Step 2 - Change the symbol from **p** to **£**.

Answer: **£9.03**

Exercise 9: 2   Write the amount as pounds:

Score

1) **351p** = _____
2) **12,068p** = _____
3) **930p** = _____
4) **525p** = _____
5) **3,884p** = _____
6) **15,192p** = _____
7) **6,417p** = _____
8) **4p** = _____
9) **673p** = _____
10) **5,206p** = _____

c. Writing Money in Full

Example: Write **£16.75** as pounds and pence.

Step 1 - The digits to the left of the decimal point are the pounds. There are **16** pounds.

Step 2 - The digits to the right of the decimal point are the pence. There are **75** pence.

Answer: **16 pounds and 75 pence**

Exercise 9: 3 Write the amount as pounds and pence:

Score

1) £0.72 is ____ pounds and ____ pence.

2) £23.69 is ____ pounds and ____ pence.

3) £125.30 is ____ pounds and ____ pence.

4) £68.99 is ____ pounds and ____ pence.

5) £104.13 is ____ pounds and ____ pence.

6) £9.62 is ____ pounds and ____ pence.

7) £13.28 is ____ pounds and ____ pence.

8) £4.56 is ____ pounds and ____ pence.

9) £55.76 is ____ pounds and ____ pence.

10) £187.05 is ____ pounds and ____ pence.

d. Writing Money in Figures

Example: Write **thirty-seven pounds and five pence** in figures.

Thirty-seven pounds comes before the decimal point and **five pence** comes after the decimal point. Write **£** before the figures.

Answer: **£37.05**

Exercise 9: 4   Write the amount in figures:

Score

1) **One hundred and three pounds and sixty-two pence is** _____ .

2) **Sixty-one pounds and forty-five pence is** _____ .

3) **One hundred and ten pounds and seventeen pence is** _____ .

4) **Two pounds and seventy-eight pence is** _____ .

5) **Twenty-nine pounds and six pence is** _____ .

6) **Zero pounds and thirty-seven pence is** _____ .

7) **Ninety-seven pounds and forty-three pence is** _____ .

8) **Eighty-six pounds and fifty-two pence is** _____ .

9) **Fifteen pounds and thirty-one pence is** _____ .

10) **One hundred pounds and eight pence is** _____ .

e. Place Value

Example: What is the value of the **3** in **£40.36**?

The amount can be displayed on a decimal table to show the place values:

T	O	t	h
4	0	3	6

The digit **3** lies in the tenths column, which represents **3** tenths of **£1**, which is **30p**.

Answer: **30p** or **£0.30**

© 2016 Stephen Curran

Exercise 9: 5 Write the value of:
(Give answers in pounds and pence.)

Score

1) the **6** in **£20.46**. _____ or _____

2) the **1** in **£130.72**. _____ or _____

3) the **8** in **£128.07**. _____ or _____

4) the **3** in **£44.32**. _____ or _____

5) the **5** in **£65.78**. _____ or _____

6) the **2** in **£180.25**. _____ or _____

7) the **9** in **£196.83**. _____ or _____

8) the **4** in **£45.62**. _____ or _____

9) the **7** in **£7.82**. _____ or _____

10) the **1** in **£30.18**. _____ or _____

f. Rounding Money

Rounding Money involves rounding to the nearest one, ten or hundred. For example:

To the nearest pound, **£3.99** would be rounded to **£4**.

Determine whether to round up or down by using the table:

Rounding to the Nearest:	Round Up	Round Down
Pound	0.5 or above	0.4 or less
Ten	5 or above	4 or less
Hundred	50 or above	49 or less

© 2016 Stephen Curran

Example: Round **£45.10** to the nearest **£10**.

If the ones are **5 or more**, **round up** to the nearest ten.
If they are **4 or less**, **round down** to the nearest ten.

Although **£45** is exactly between **£40** and **£50**, **5** always rounds up to the next multiple of ten. This means **£45** to the nearest **£10** will round up to **£50**.

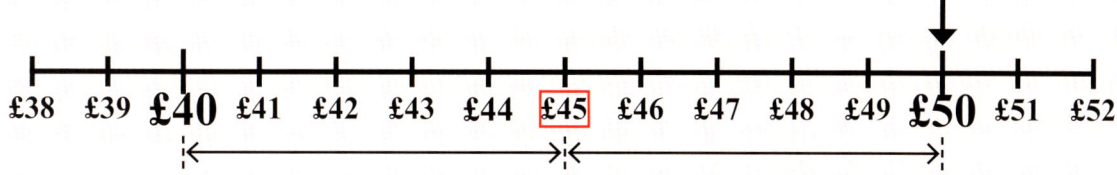

Answer: **£50**

Exercise 9: 6 Round the amount:

To the nearest **pound**:

1) £1.25 _____   2) £2.78 _____

To the nearest **five pounds**:

3) £26.32 _____   4) £7.28 _____

To the nearest **£10**:

5) £28.16 _____   6) £43.50 _____

To the nearest **£50**:

7) £128.30 _____   8) £76.80 _____

To the nearest **£100**:

9) £192.97 _____   10) £72.13 _____

3. Notes & Coinage

There are eight commonly used coins and four banknotes in the United Kingdom. The values of each coin or banknote can be combined to make any amount.

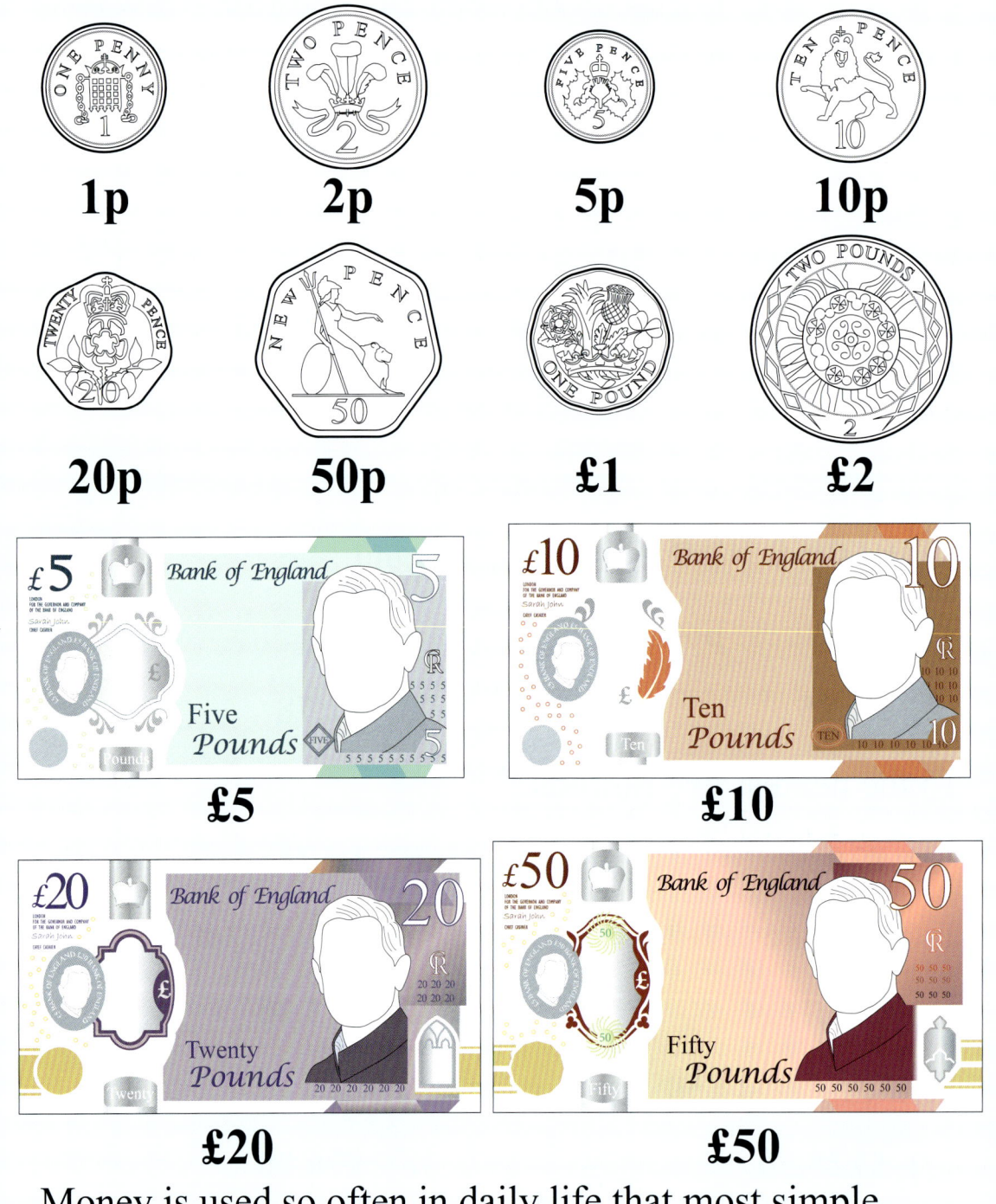

Money is used so often in daily life that most simple calculations can be done mentally. The values of notes and coins are designed to be counted quickly so they can be easily used to pay for goods and services.

a. Counting Money

Example: What is the total value of these notes and coins?

£20   £10

£2   20p   10p   5p   1p

Write the value of each note and coin and add them together.

£20 + £10 + £2 + 20p + 10p + 5p + 1p = £32.36

Answer: **£32.36**

Exercise 9: 7

What is the total value of the notes and coins?

Score

1) £20
   £1   10p   5p

2) £10   50p
   £5   £2

3) £5   50p
   £1   20p   1p

4) £10   £2
   £1   5p   2p   1p

5) £20, £2, £5, 50p, 20p, 10p

_____

6) £10, £2, £5, £1, 50p, 2p

_____

7) £5, 20p, £5, 10p

_____

8) £20, £2, £1, 2p, 1p

_____

9) £5, £1, £2, £2, 50p, 20p, 5p, 5p, 5p, 2p

_____

10) £20, £2, £2, £20, 50p, £10, 5p

_____

b. Least Number of Notes & Coins

Example: Which notes and coins make up **£27.17**, using the least number of notes and coins?

Begin with the largest value of note that will fit into **£27.17**, then work down the cash values to make up the amount.

The largest note is **£20**, followed by **£5**, then **£2**, then **10p**, then **5p** and **2p**. Add the values along the way.

£20 + £5 + £2 + 10p + 5p + 2p = £27.17

Answer: **£20, £5, £2, 10p, 5p and 2p**

Exercise 9: 8

Which notes and coins make up the amount, using the least number of notes and coins?

Score

1) **£12.50** = ____ ____ ____
2) **£8.76** = ____ ____ ____ ____ ____ ____ ____
3) **£26.10** = ____ ____ ____ ____
4) **£17.25** = ____ ____ ____ ____ ____
5) **£20.13** = ____ ____ ____ ____
6) **£11.27** = _____
7) **£32.63** = _____
8) **£25.80** = _____
9) **£6.08** = _____
10) **£38.88** = _____

c. Finding Change in Amounts

Example: What change would be given from **£5** if **£1.68** is spent?

A number line can help show the leftover amount.

Step 1 - Count from **£1.68** to the nearest whole pound, which is **£2**. The difference is **32p**.

Step 2 - Count from **£2** to **£5** which is **£3**.

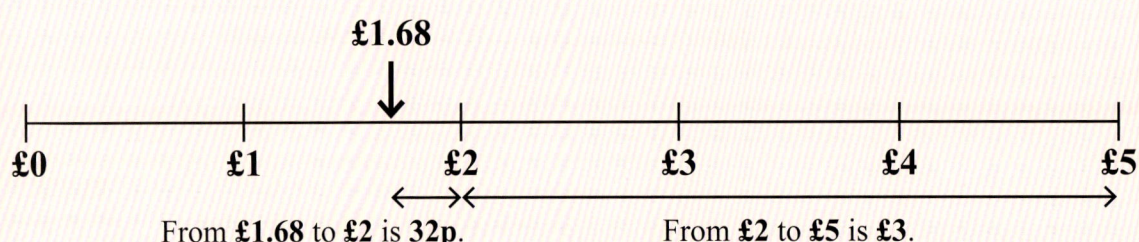

Step 3 - Combine the two amounts to find the total change.
32p + £3 = £3.32

Answer: **£3.32**

Exercise 9: 9

How much change would be given if this amount is spent?

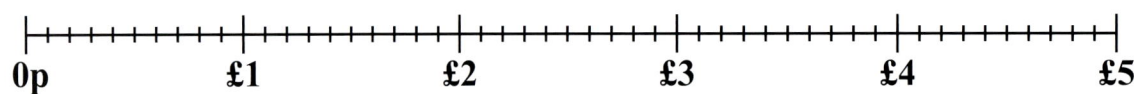

From a **£5** note:

1) **£3.29** _____   2) **£1.58** _____

3) **£4.61** _____   4) **£0.73** _____

5) **£2.17** _____

From a **£10** note:

6) **£5.96** _____   7) **£7.89** _____

8) **£3.78** _____   9) **£0.42** _____

10) **£6.25** _____

Score

d. Finding Change in Cash

Example: What change in notes and coins would be given from a **£20** note if **£14.74** is spent?

Step 1 - Add the smallest amount of coins to **£14.74** to make it up to **£15**. Begin with the smallest coin value, then work up the coin values to make up the amount using the least amount of coins possible.

£14.74 + (1p) = £14.75

£14.75 + (5p) = £14.80   Add the values along the way.

£14.80 + (20p) = £15.00

£14.74 + 1p + 5p + 20p = £15

The change so far is **26p**.

Step 2 - Add the smallest number of notes to **£15** to make it up to **£20**. This will be a **£5** note.

£5

Answer: **1p**, **5p**, **20p** and **£5**

© 2016 Stephen Curran

Exercise 9: 10

How much change in notes and coins would be given if this amount is spent (use the least number of notes and coins)?

From a **£2** coin:

1) **£1.62** _____   2) **£0.53** _____

From a **£5** note:

3) **£2.17** _____   4) **£3.85** _____

From a **£10** note:

5) **£4.81** _____   6) **£7.64** _____

From a **£20** note:

7) **£9.49** _____   8) **£11.47** _____

From a **£50** note:

9) **£12.44** _____   10) **£33.69** _____

Score

4. Money Calculations

More complex **Money Calculations** involving the Four Rules of Number are best solved using paper and pen methods.

a. Adding Money

The rules for **Adding** money are the same as Decimal Addition:
1. Keep the decimal points in line.
2. Fill all the empty spaces with **zeros**.
3. Add as normal using standard column addition.

Example: Calculate **£36.70 + £12.56 + 87p**.

Step 1 - Set out the calculation in column format. The pence must be converted to pounds. Keep the decimal points in line.

Step 2 - Fill in all the empty spaces with **zeros**.

Step 3 - Add as normal.

Answer: **£50.13**

```
  £ 3 6 . 7 0
  £ 1 2 . 5 6
  £ 0 0 . 8 7 +
  ─────────────
  £ 3 6 . 7 0
  £ 1 2 . 5 6
  £ 0 0 . 8 7 +
  ─────────────
  £ 5 0 . 1 3
       1 2   1
```

Exercise 9: 11   Set out and calculate:

1) £54.62 + £12.13

   £ 5 4 . 6 2
   £ 1 2 . 1 3 +
   ─────────────

2) £138.16 + £14.67

   £ 1 3 8 . 1 6
   £ 0 1 4 . 6 7 +
   ─────────────

3) £77.94 + £23.28

4) £75.07 + £60.21

5) £129.72 + 13p

6) £81.45 + £46.39

7) £139.50 + £54.89 + £7.22   8) £61.31 + £19.07 + £5.95

_____ +
_____

_____ +
_____

9) £128.63 + £42.48 + 80p   10) £173.74 + £86.19 + 56p

_____ +
_____

_____ +
_____

b. Subtracting Money

The rules for **Subtracting** money are the same as Decimal Subtraction:

1. Keep the decimal points in line.
2. Fill all the empty spaces with **zeros**.
3. Subtract as normal using standard column subtraction.

Example: Calculate £72.19 – £8.86.

Step 1 - Set out the calculation in column format, keeping the decimal points in line.

$$\begin{array}{r} £72.19 \\ £8.86 - \\ \hline \end{array}$$

Step 2 - Fill in all empty spaces with **zeros**.

Step 3 - Subtract as normal.

$$\begin{array}{r} £\cancel{7}^6\cancel{2}^1.^1 9 \\ £08.86 - \\ \hline £63.33 \end{array}$$

Answer: **£63.33**

Exercise 9: 12   Set out and calculate:

1) £32.26 – £3.05

2) £77.19 – £18.57

£ 3 2 . 2 6
£ 0 3 . 0 5 –

£ 7 7 . 1 9
£ 1 8 . 5 7 –

3) £96.32 – £56.70

4) £105.44 – £24.81

5) £49.98 – £32.61

6) £86.79 – £60.01

7) £192.72 – £81.05

8) £99.25 – £17.86

9) £171.10 − £64.47   10) £142.50 − £58.93

c. Multiplying Money

When **Multiplying Money**, simply multiply as normal using standard column multiplication. Be careful to write the decimal point and keep it in line in the answer.

Note: multiplying money is the same as repeated addition. For example, **£1.50 × 3 = £1.50 + £1.50 + £1.50 = £4.50**

Example: Calculate £107.24 × 5.

Step 1 - Set out the calculation as a standard short column multiplication.

$$\begin{array}{r} £107.24 \\ 5\times \\ \hline \end{array}$$

Step 2 - Multiply as normal. Be careful to keep the decimal point in line in the answer.

$$\begin{array}{r} £107.24 \\ 5\times \\ \hline £536.20 \\ \end{array}$$
_{3 1 2}

Answer: **£536.20**

Exercise 9: 13 Set out and calculate:

Score

1) £19.37 × 2

```
£ 1 9 . 3 7
        2 ×
_____
          .
_____
```

2) £43.91 × 5

```
£ 4 3 . 9 1
        5 ×
_____
          .
_____
```

3) £65.24 × 3

4) £121.46 × 6

5) £188.62 × 4

6) £34.13 × 7

7) £57.80 × 9

8) £76.58 × 5

9) £102.75 × 8   10) £90.09 × 9

            ×   ×
    _____   _____

    _____   _____

d. Dividing Money

Example: How many **20p** coins are in **£24**?

Step 1 - Think of how many **20p** coins will make up **£1**.

There are **five 20p** coins because:
20p × 5 = 100p = £1

Step 2 - Multiply by **24** to work out how many **20p** coins are in **£24**.

24 × 5 = 120 coins
So, if **£24** is divided by **20p**, the answer is **120**.

$$\begin{array}{r} 2\,4 \\ 5\times \\ \hline 1\,2\,0 \\ {\scriptstyle 2} \end{array}$$

Answer: **120**

Exercise 9: 14   How many: Score

1) **10p** coins are in **£15**? ____   2) **10p** coins are in **£28**? ____

3) **20p** coins are in **£36**? ____   4) **20p** coins are in **£44**? ____

5) **20p** coins are in **£21**? ____   6) **20p** coins are in **£17**? ____

7) **50p** coins are in **£16**? ____   8) **50p** coins are in **£25**? ____

9) **50p** coins are in **£39**? ____ 10) **50p** coins are in **£50**? ____

When **Dividing Money**, simply divide as normal using standard short division. Be careful to write the decimal point and keep it in line in the answer.

Example: Calculate **£68.52 ÷ 4**.

Step 1 - Set out the calculation as a standard short division.

$$4\overline{)£68.52}$$

Step 2 - Divide, keeping the decimal point in line in the answer.

$$4\overline{)£6^28.5^12} = £17.13$$

Answer: **£17.13**

Exercise 9: 15   Set out and calculate:

1) **£162.52 ÷ 2**   2) **£8.01 ÷ 3**

$$2\overline{)£162.52}$$ $$3\overline{)£8.01}$$

3) **£84.70 ÷ 5**   4) **£82.08 ÷ 8**

5) **£93.60 ÷ 3**   6) **£33.24 ÷ 6**

7) £16.36 ÷ 4

8) £143.08 ÷ 7

9) £172.35 ÷ 9

10) £100.60 ÷ 5

Example: What is $\frac{1}{6}$ of **£15.24**?

Step 1 - Finding $\frac{1}{6}$ of an amount is the same as dividing by **6**.

$6\overline{)£15.24}$

Set out the calculation as a standard short division by **6**.

Step 2 - Divide, keeping the decimal point in line in the answer.

$6\overline{)£1^15.^32^24}$ = £02.54

Answer: **£2.54**

Exercise 9: 16   Find:

1) $\frac{1}{2}$ of **£62.84**. _____
2) $\frac{1}{10}$ of **£30.50**. _____
3) $\frac{1}{3}$ of **£92.73**. _____
4) $\frac{1}{7}$ of **£3.43**. _____
5) $\frac{1}{5}$ of **£187.35**. _____
6) $\frac{1}{8}$ of **£158.56**. _____
7) $\frac{1}{6}$ of **£49.50**. _____
8) $\frac{1}{9}$ of **£73.08**. _____
9) $\frac{1}{4}$ of **£156**. _____
10) $\frac{1}{12}$ of **£24.12**. _____

5. Fractional Costs

Finding **Fractional Costs** is the same as finding fractional parts. For example, $\frac{3}{4}$ of **£20** is **£15**.

$$\frac{3}{4} \text{ of } £20 = £15$$

Example: Find $\frac{3}{5}$ of **£15.60**.

Step 1 - Find the value of $\frac{1}{5}$.
Divide the amount by the denominator.

£15.60 ÷ 5 = £3.12

$$\begin{array}{r} £\,0\,3\,.\,1\,2 \\ 5\,\overline{)£\,1\,5\,.\,6\,0} \end{array}$$

Step 2 - Find the value of $\frac{3}{5}$.
Multiply by the numerator.

£3.12 × 3 = £9.36

$$\begin{array}{r} £\,3\,.\,1\,2 \\ 3\,\times \\ \hline £\,9\,.\,3\,6 \end{array}$$

Answer: **£9.36**

Exercise 9: 17   Find:  Score

1) $\frac{2}{3}$ of **£98.67**. _____
2) $\frac{3}{4}$ of **£125.60**. _____
3) $\frac{5}{8}$ of **£146.56**. _____
4) $\frac{2}{9}$ of **£41.31**. _____
5) $\frac{5}{6}$ of **£112.74**. _____
6) $\frac{2}{5}$ of **£140.35**. _____
7) $\frac{3}{7}$ of **£78.61**. _____
8) $\frac{7}{8}$ of **£74.96**. _____
9) $\frac{4}{9}$ of **£182.52**. _____
10) $\frac{5}{7}$ of **£53.06**. _____

6. Money in Words

Below is a reminder of the different words used to describe the Four Rules of Number:

Add	Subtract	Multiply	Divide
Plus	Less	Find the product of	Share
Total	Minus	Multiply	Divide
Increase	Take away/from	Times	Find the quotient
Combine	Deduct	Double/Twice (×2)	Partition
Altogether	Decrease	Treble/Triple (×3)	Separate into
Find the sum of	Find the difference	Quadruple (×4)	Split into

Example: Share **one hundred and sixty-one pounds and fourteen pence** by **seven**.

Step 1 - 'Share' means divide, so write the number sentence:

£161.14 ÷ 7

Step 2 - Complete using standard short division:

$$\begin{array}{r} £\,0\,2\,3\,.\,0\,2 \\ 7\overline{)£\,1^{1}6^{2}1\,.\,1^{1}4} \end{array}$$

Answer: **£23.02**

Exercise 9: 18 Answer the following:

Score

1) Increase **thirty-eight pounds and seventy-five pence** by **eight pounds and fifty-six pence**. _____

2) Share **one hundred and eighty-two pounds and twelve pence** by **four**. _____

3) Find the product of **fifty-two pence** and **five**. _____

4) What is **one hundred and thirteen pounds and sixteen pence** minus **fifteen pounds and twenty-seven pence**? _____

5) What is **twenty-three pounds and four pence** divided by **eight**? _____

6) Combine **one hundred and thirty-eight pounds and fifty pence** and **eighty-four pounds and thirty-five pence**. _____

7) Multiply **one pound and sixty-eight pence** by **seven**. _____

8) Find the difference between **one hundred and sixty-five pounds and seventy pence** and **thirty-nine pounds and forty pence**. _____

9) Find the sum of **eighty-seven pounds and forty-three pence** and **thirty-one pounds and fourteen pence**. _____

10) Quadruple **one hundred and seventeen pounds**. _____

7. Problem Solving

Example: A group of **four** friends go to a theme park. A group ticket costs **£31**. Individual tickets (for one person) cost **£8.75** each. How much will the friends save with a group ticket?

Step 1 - Find the total cost of **four** individual tickets by multiplying.
£8.75 × 4 = £35

```
   £ 8 . 7 5
         4 ×
   ─────────
   £ 3 5 . 0 0
       3 2
```

Step 2 - Subtract to find the difference in price.
£35 − £31 = £4

Answer: **£4**

Exercise 9: 19   Answer the following:

1) How much is in this money box? _____

50p	20p	10p	5p	2p	1p
3	2	1	2	2	3

2) A family of **2** adults and **2** children go to the cinema. It costs **£5.50** for an adult ticket and **£1.25** less for a child ticket. How much does it cost the whole family to go to the cinema? _____

3) A pack of **10** pencils costs **50p**. How much does **70** pencils cost? _____

4) Millie wants to buy her sister a teddy bear for her birthday. The teddy costs **£15**. Millie is given **£1.50** pocket money per week. For how many weeks does she need to save? _____

5) Adam has **£5.10**, his brother James has **£1.20** more than him. Their friend, Lee, has double what James has. How much money does Lee have? _____

6) Lily gets the bus every weekday. The bus costs **£1.50** a day. If Lily's mum gives her a **£10** note, how much change does she have at the end of the week? _____

7) A birthday party costs **£13.50** per child. If Johnny invites **8** friends, what is the total cost of the party? _____

8) Kajal buys **6** sets of pens. She receives **£1.64** change from a **£5** note. How much did each set cost? _____

9) In a half-price sale, Harry's parents buy him a bicycle for **£53.75**. What was its original price? _____

10) To take his family of **four** on holiday, Mr Cartwright needs to save **£175.20** per person. How much does he need to save per week if he has **8** weeks to save? _____

Score

Chapter Ten
MEASUREMENT
1. Metric Measurements

Metric Measurements are based on the Tens Number System. There are four types of measurement:
- **Distance** - the length of something
- **Weight** - how heavy something is
- **Capacity** - how much space is inside something
- **Temperature** - how hot or cold something is

Metric measurements use the following common descriptions. 'Milli' is the smallest and 'kilo' is the largest.

Milli	$\frac{1}{1000}$	One-thousandth
Centi	$\frac{1}{100}$	One-hundredth
Kilo	1,000	One Thousand

a. Distance

Distance is the measurement of how long something is. Units of distance measurement from smallest to largest are:
- **millimetres** or **mm**
- **centimetres** or **cm**
- **metres** or **m**
- **kilometres** or **km**

Measurements can be written in, or converted to, any of the above forms. Some important conversions are listed below:

```
10 millimetres (mm)      = 1 centimetre (cm)
1,000 millimetres (mm)   = 1 metre (m)
100 centimetres (cm)     = 1 metre (m)
1,000 metres (m)         = 1 kilometre (km)
```

> Example: Change **4** metres (m) to millimetres (mm).
>
> **Step 1** - Use the distance conversions box to check how many millimetres are in a metre.
>
> 1 metre (m) = **1,000** millimetres (mm)
>
> **Step 2** - Multiply by **4** to find **4** metres in millimetres.
>
> 1,000 × 4 = 4,000
>
> Answer: **4,000 millimetres** (or **4,000mm**)

Exercise 10: 1   Calculate the following:

Score

1) **130mm** = _____ cm
2) **200cm** = _____ m
3) **3,000mm** = _____ m
4) **2,000m** = _____ km
5) **5cm** = _____ mm
6) **4m** = _____ cm
7) **5m** = _____ mm
8) **3km** = _____ m
9) **250mm** = _____ cm
10) **6,000mm** = _____ m

Distances should be measured in the most suitable unit. Examples of everyday objects are given below for each unit of measurement, making it easier to judge the correct unit:

1 millimetre or **1mm**	**1 centimetre** or **1cm**	**1 metre** or **1m**	**1 kilometre** or **1km**
		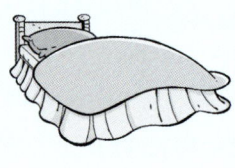	
Roughly the thickness of a credit card.	Roughly the width of a finger.	Roughly the width of a single bed.	Roughly the distance travelled in a 12-minute walk.

> Example: What unit would be used to measure the distance between two towns?
>
> The distance between two towns is more than a 12-minute walk, so the best unit of measurement is kilometres (km).
>
> Answer: **kilometres (km)**

Exercise 10: 2 What unit would be used to measure:
1) the length of a pencil? _____
2) the distance between two villages? _____
3) the width of a table? _____
4) the height of a chair? _____
5) the length of a river? _____
6) the height of a tower? _____
7) the length of a piece of paper? _____
8) the height of an adult? _____
9) the thickness of a calculator? _____
10) the thickness of a book? _____

Score

b. Weight

Weight is the measurement of how heavy something is. Units of weight measurement from smallest to largest are:
- **grams** or **g**
- **kilograms** or **kg**
- **tonnes** or **t**

Measurements can be written in, or converted to, any of the above forms. Some important conversions are listed below:

```
1,000 milligrams (mg) = 1 gram (g)
1,000 grams (g)       = 1 kilogram (kg)
1,000 kilograms (kg)  = 1 tonne (t)
```

Example: How many grams (g) are in **2** kilograms (kg)?

Step 1 - Use the weight conversions box to check how many grams are in a kilogram.

1,000 grams (g) = **1** kilogram (kg)

Step 2 - Multiply by **2** to find **2** kilograms in grams.

1,000 × **2** = **2,000**

Answer: **2,000 grams** (or **2,000g**)

Exercise 10: 3   Calculate the following:

1) **2,000mg** = _____ g   2) **10,000g** = _____ kg

3) **7,000kg** = _____ t   4) **3,000g** = _____ kg

5) **8g** = _____ mg   6) **4t** = _____ kg

7) **5kg** = _____ g   8) **6,000g** = _____ kg

9) **11,000mg** = _____ g   10) **9,000kg** = _____ t

Weight should be measured in the most suitable unit. Examples of the weights of everyday objects are given below for each unit of measurement, making it easier to judge the correct unit:

1 gram or **1g**   **1 kilogram** or **1kg**   **1 tonne** or **1t**

Roughly the weight of a paperclip.   Roughly the weight of a bag of sugar.   Roughly the weight of a rhinoceros.

Example: What unit would be used to measure the weight of a computer?

The weight of a computer would be more than the weight of a bag of sugar but much less than a rhinoceros, so the best unit of measurement is kilograms (kg).

Answer: **kilograms (kg)**

Exercise 10: 4 What unit would be used to measure:
1) the weight of a bag of flour? _____
2) the weight of a packet of crisps? _____
3) the weight of an elephant? _____
4) the weight of a cat? _____
5) the weight of a book? _____
6) the weight of a printer? _____
7) the weight of a cake? _____
8) the weight of a letter? _____
9) the weight of a truck? _____
10) the weight of a phone? _____

Score

c. Capacity

Capacity is the measurement of how much space is inside something. Units of capacity measurement from smallest to largest are:
- **millilitres** or **mℓ**
- **centilitres** or **cℓ**
- **litres** or **ℓ**

Measurements can be written in, or converted to, any of the above forms. Some important conversions are listed below:

10 millilitres (mℓ)   = **1** centilitre (cℓ)
1,000 millilitres (mℓ) = **1** litre (ℓ)
100 centilitres (cℓ) = **1** litre (ℓ)

Example: Convert **6** litres (ℓ) to centilitres (cℓ)?

Step 1 - Use the capacity conversions box to check how many centilitres are in a litre.

1 litre (ℓ) = **100** centilitres (cℓ)

Step 2 - Multiply by **6** to find **6** litres in centilitres.

100 × 6 = 600

Answer: **600 centilitres** (or **600cℓ**)

Exercise 10: 5   Calculate the following:

Score

1) **6,000mℓ** = _____ ℓ
2) **200cℓ** = _____ ℓ
3) **30mℓ** = _____ cℓ
4) **50mℓ** = _____ cℓ
5) **4ℓ** = _____ mℓ
6) **7ℓ** = _____ cℓ
7) **9cℓ** = _____ mℓ
8) **10,000mℓ** = _____ ℓ
9) **80mℓ** = _____ cℓ
10) **1,100cℓ** = _____ ℓ

Capacity should be measured in the most suitable unit. Examples of the capacities of everyday objects are given below for each unit of measurement, making it easier to judge the correct unit:

1 millilitre or **1mℓ**

1 centilitre or **1cℓ**

1 litre or **1ℓ**

Roughly 20 raindrops in capacity.

Roughly a dessertspoon in capacity.

Roughly a jug of water in capacity.

© 2016 Stephen Curran

Example: What unit would be used to measure the capacity of a thimble?

The capacity of a thimble would be less than the capacity of a dessertspoon, so the best unit of measurement is millilitres (ml).

Answer: **millilitres (ml)**

Exercise 10: 6 What unit would be used to measure:

1) the capacity of a teacup? _____
2) the capacity of a teaspoon? _____
3) the capacity of a kettle? _____
4) the capacity of a plant pot? _____
5) the capacity of a glass? _____
6) the capacity of a pan? _____
7) the capacity of a can? _____
8) the capacity of a bowl? _____
9) the capacity of a carton? _____
10) the capacity of a bucket? _____

Score

2. Metric Conversions

A metric measurement can be expressed in a number of ways using different units of measurement. For example, all the amounts below are equal to each other.

metres		centimetres		millimetres		centimetres & millimetres
0.074m	=	**7.4cm**	=	**74mm**	=	**7cm 4mm**

It is important to be able to convert from each form to another. This can be difficult when moving from the largest unit to the smallest unit and vice versa.

Conversion Factors are needed for metric conversions. A conversion factor is the number that is either multiplied or divided by in order to change the unit of measurement. For example, to move from **7.4cm** to **74mm** there is a conversion factor of **10** (multiply by **10**).

Note: It is very important to learn these conversions.

Length
10 millimetres (mm) = 1 centimetre (cm)
1,000 millimetres (mm) = 1 metre (m)
100 centimetres (cm) = 1 metre (m)
1,000 metres (m) = 1 kilometre (km)

Weight
1,000 milligrams (mg) = 1 gram (g)
1,000 grams (g) = 1 kilogram (kg)
1,000 kilograms (kg) = 1 tonne (t)

Capacity
10 millilitres (mℓ) = 1 centilitre (cℓ)
1,000 millilitres (mℓ) = 1 litre (ℓ)
100 centilitres (cℓ) = 1 litre (ℓ)

Four-step Conversion Method

Example: Change **2.8** metres to centimetres.

Step 1 - Find the conversion factor by asking this question.

How many <u>smaller metric units</u> are in the <u>larger metric unit</u>?

In this case - how many <u>centimetres</u> are in <u>one metre</u>?

The conversion factor is: **100cm** in **1m**.

Step 2 - Is the unit being broken up into smaller pieces or joined up into larger pieces?

If the original amount is moving to smaller units,

it is being broken up. If it is moving to larger units, it is being joined up.

Metres to centimetres is breaking up.

Step 3 - Are there more or less pieces? If the original amount is broken up, there will be more pieces. If it is joined up, there will be less pieces.

Metres to centimetres is more pieces.

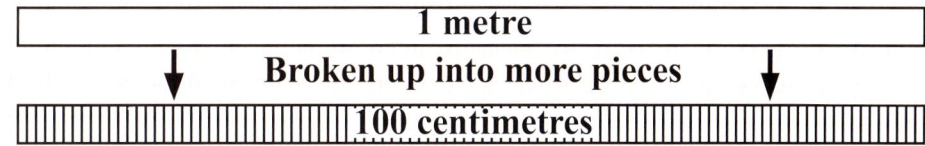

Step 4 - Move the decimal point by the number of **zeros** in the conversion factor.

If there are more pieces move the point to the right; if there are less pieces move the point to the left.

2 zeros means move the decimal point 2 places to the right.

2 places right

$$2.8 \times 100 = 280.0 = 280$$

Answer: **280cm**

Exercise 10: 7   Calculate the following:

1) **20mℓ** = _____ cℓ
2) **5,000m** = _____ km
3) **5,000g** = _____ kg
4) **7cm** = _____ mm
5) **9,000mm** = _____ m
6) **6ℓ** = _____ cℓ
7) **8ℓ** = _____ mℓ
8) **1,000cm** = _____ m
9) **4,000kg** = _____ t
10) **10,000mg** = _____ g

3. Decimal Measurements

Decimal Measurements can be split into two separate units of measurement.

For example:

7.5kg could be written as **7 kilograms and 500 grams**.

An easy error would be to write this amount as **7 kilograms and 5 grams** and not realise that **0.5** is half a kilogram and must be written as **500** grams.

Example: Write **3.82ℓ** in litres and millilitres.

Step 1 - The digits to the left of the decimal point can be written as litres. There are **3** litres.

Step 2 - As there are **1,000** millilitres in a litre, **3.82ℓ** could be written as **3.820ℓ**. This means there are **820** millilitres.

Answer: **3 litres and 820 millilitres**

Exercise 10: 8   Fill in the equivalent amount:

1) **5.2cm**   = _____ cm and _____ mm

2) **10.68g**   = _____ g and _____ mg

3) **4.3ℓ**   = _____ ℓ and _____ mℓ

4) **2.56m**   = _____ m and _____ mm

5) **6.19t**   = _____ t and _____ kg

6) **1.7cℓ**   = _____ cℓ and _____ mℓ

7) **8.05km** = _____km and _____m

8) **9.8ℓ** = _____ℓ and _____cℓ

9) **3.93kg** = _____kg and _____g

10) **7.4m** = _____m and _____cm

Score

Example: Write **3 kilograms and 25 grams** in kilograms.

Step 1 - **3** kilograms can be written to the left of the decimal point as **3.0**.

Step 2 - As there are **1,000** grams in **1** kilogram, **25** grams must be changed to **0.025** kilograms.

Answer: **3.025 kilograms**

Exercise 10: 9 Fill in the equivalent amount:

1) **3km and 37m** = _____km

2) **5ℓ and 175mℓ** = _____ℓ

3) **8cm and 9mm** = _____cm

4) **7kg and 250g** = _____kg

5) **10m and 680mm** = _____m

6) **1g and 954mg** = _____g

7) **6ℓ and 71cℓ** = _____ℓ

8) **9t and 320kg** = _____t

9) **4m and 4cm** = _____m

10) **2cℓ and 3mℓ** = _____cℓ

Score

4. Reading Metric Scales
a. Measuring Distance

Rulers are usually marked up in metric and imperial units. One side of the ruler is measured in metres, centimetres and millimetres (metric units):

10 millimetres = **1** centimetre
100 centimetres = **1** metre

Most rulers, like the one below, are shorter than **1** metre.

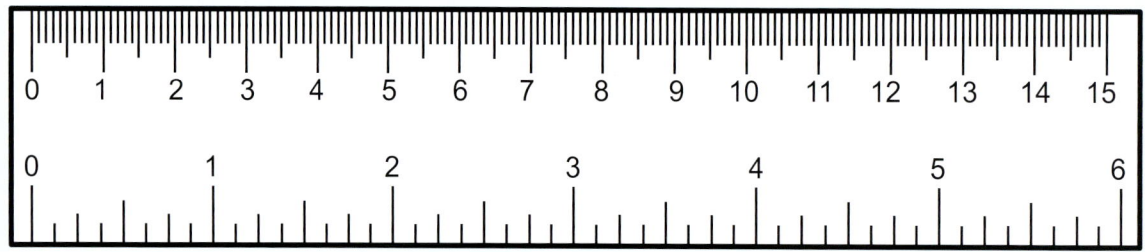

The other side of the ruler is measured in inches (imperial units). These inches are divided into eighths.

There are **12** inches to **one** foot. This is a **6** inch ruler.

Note: **6** inches is approximately **15** centimetres.
12 inches is approximately **30** centimetres.

Metric measurements are more commonly used.

Example: What measurement is the arrow pointing to on the ruler? Give the answer in centimetres and in millimetres.

The arrow points to **3cm and 4mm**. This can be written as **3.4cm** or **34mm**.

Answer: **3.4cm** or **34mm**

Exercise 10: 10 What measurement is the arrow pointing to on the ruler? Give the answer in centimetres and in millimetres.

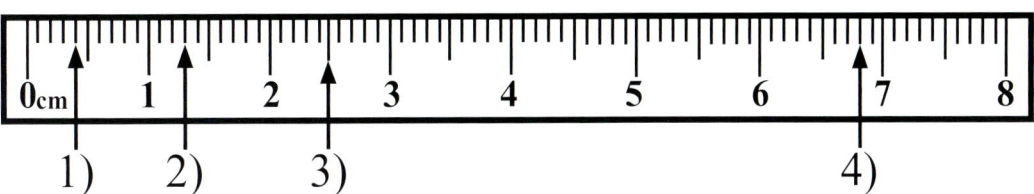

1) _____ cm or _____ mm   2) _____ cm or _____ mm
3) _____ cm or _____ mm   4) _____ cm or _____ mm

Use a ruler to measure the line:

5) _____ cm or _____ mm   6) _____ cm or _____ mm

7) _____ cm or _____ mm   8) _____ cm or _____ mm

9) _____ cm or _____ mm   10) _____ cm or _____ mm

b. Measuring Weight

Scales are used to **Measure Weight**.

They are marked up in grams and kilograms according to the maximum amount they are measuring. This means there are various types of weight scales, such as bathroom scales, kitchen scales, etc.

Old-fashioned scales used two balancing sides to measure equal weight.

Modern scales are usually mechanical or electronic.

Example: What measurement is the arrow pointing to on the scales? Give the answer in grams and in kilograms.

These scales are marked up into **10kg** sections, with a further division into **5kg** sections.

This means the arrow points to **20kg** and **5kg** which is **25kg**. This can be written as **25,000g** or **25kg**.

Answer: **25,000g** or **25kg**

Exercise 10: 11

What weight do the scales show? Give the answer in kilograms and in grams.

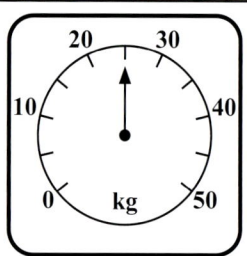
Score

1) ____kg or ____g

2) ____kg or ____g

3) ____kg or ____g

4) ____kg or ____g

5) ____kg or ____g

6) ____kg or ____g

42   © 2016 Stephen Curran

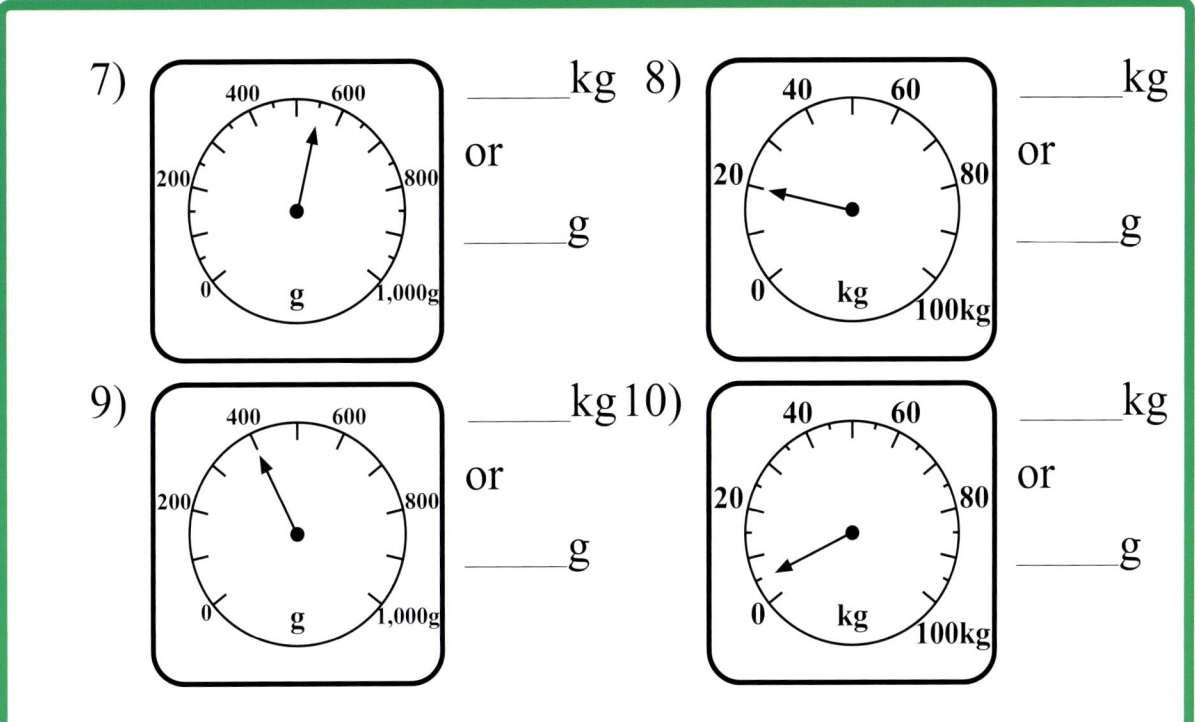

7) _____kg or _____g
8) _____kg or _____g
9) _____kg or _____g
10) _____kg or _____g

Balancing scales (pair of scales) are a type of weighing device.

They have a balance beam and two dishes and work in a similar way to a see-saw.

To measure an object's weight, it is placed in one dish and standard weights are placed in the other dish until the scales balance. This means both sides contain exactly the same weight.

Examples of standard weights are shown below:

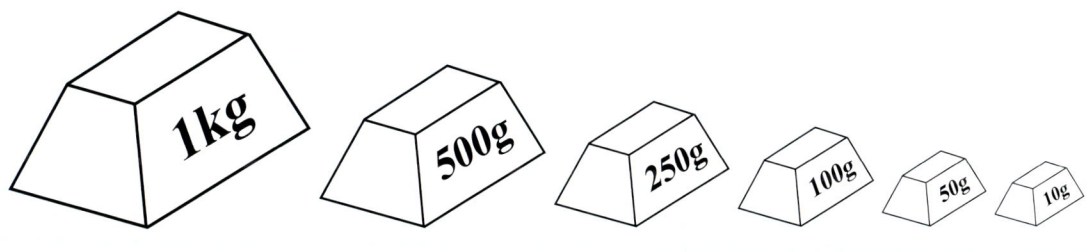

Example: What weights will make the scales balance?

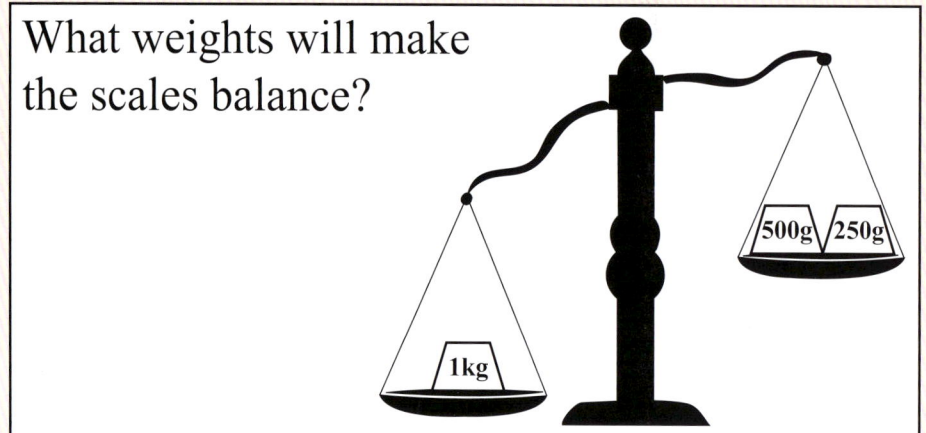

Step 1 - The lower side of the scales is the heavier side and weighs **1kg**.

Step 2 - The higher and lighter side weighs **750g**.

Step 3 - Subtract to find the difference between the two sides. **1kg – 750g = 250g**

Step 4 - Starting with the largest possible weight, work out which weights will make up **250g**. This is **250g**.

Answer: **250g**

Exercise 10: 12

What weights will make the scales balance (use the smallest amount of weights possible)?

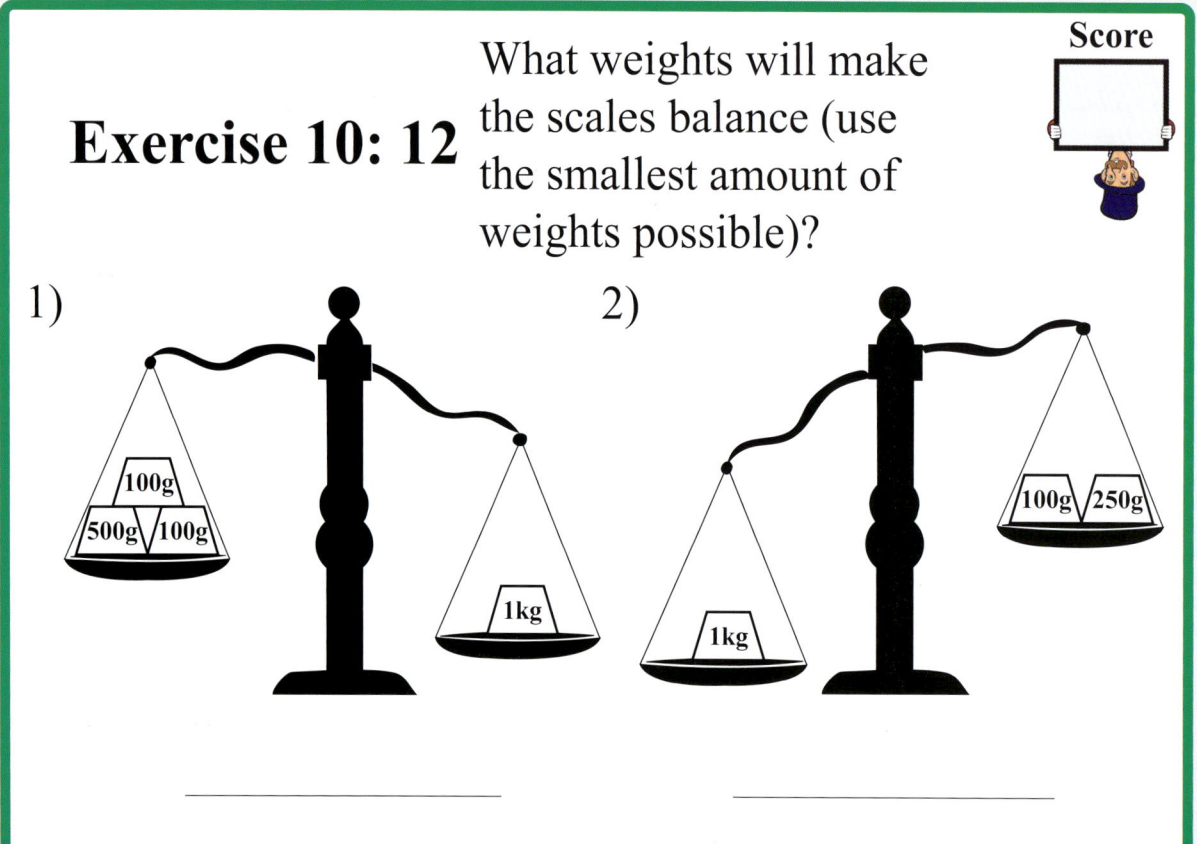

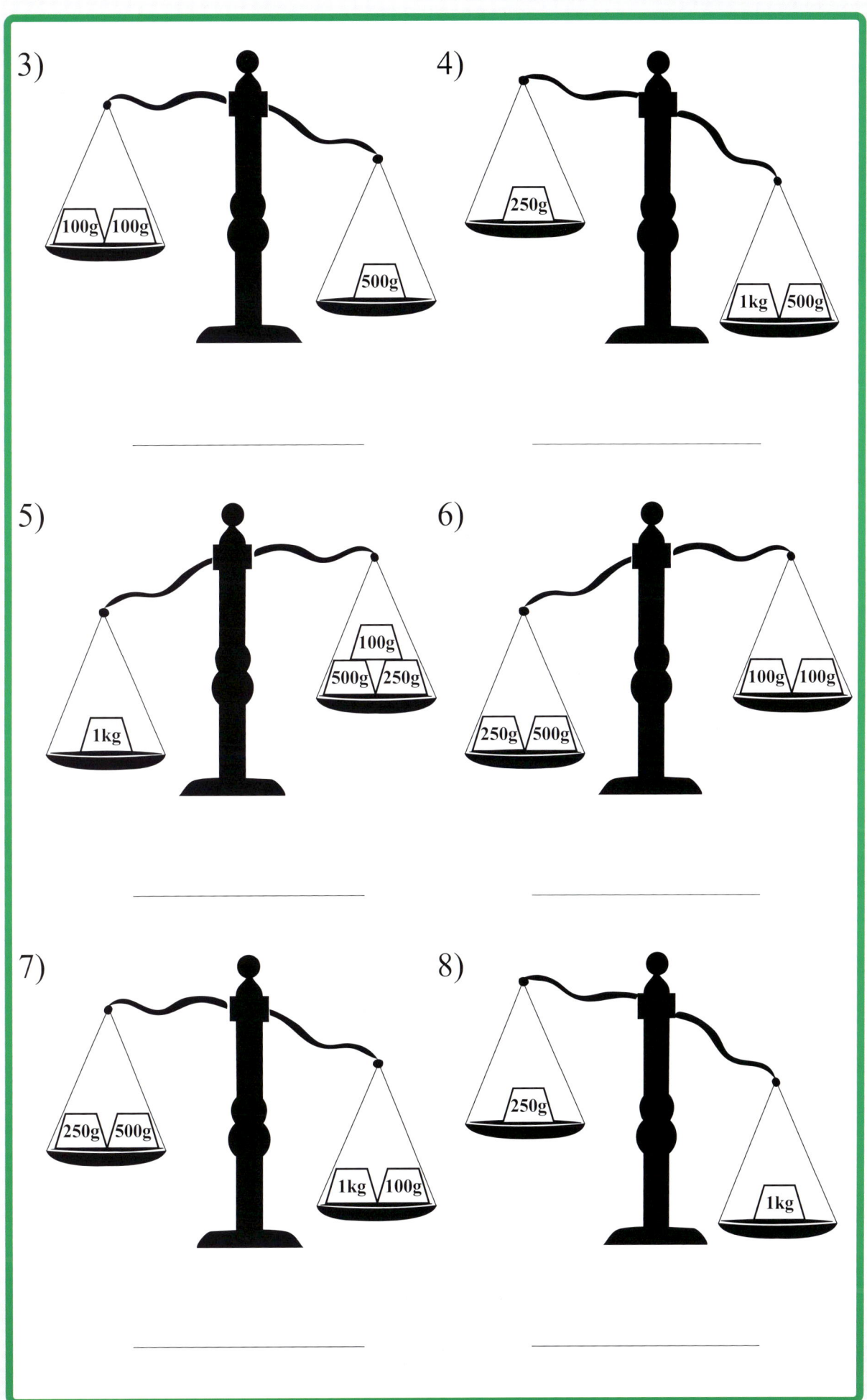

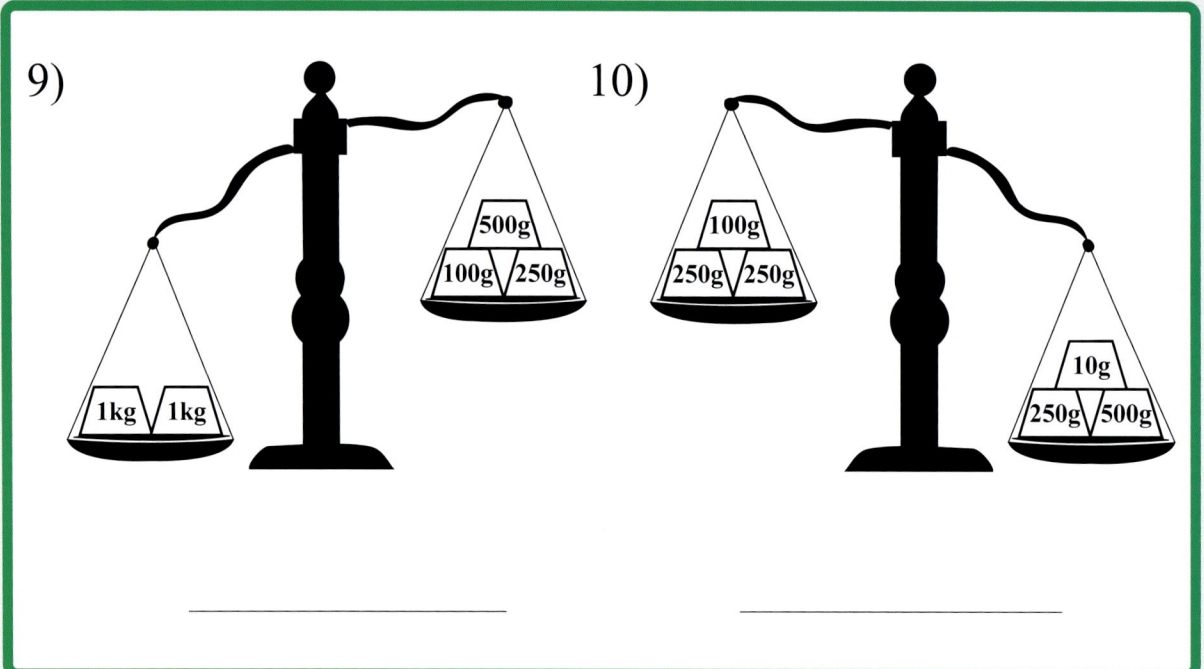

c. Measuring Capacity

Capacity is measured using measuring jugs or beakers, which are normally used to measure liquids.

They are marked up in millilitres, centilitres and litres according to the maximum amount they are measuring. These markings usually appear on the outside of the measuring device.

Example: What amount does this beaker contain?

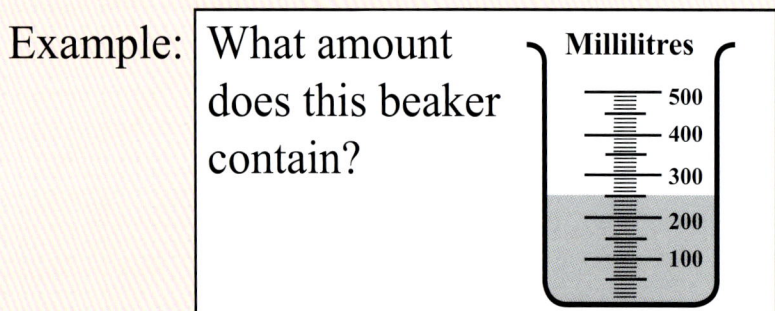

Each marking on the beaker represents **10ml**. This means the level of the liquid reaches **250ml**.

Answer: **250ml**

Exercise 10: 13

What amount does the beaker contain?

Score

1) Litres 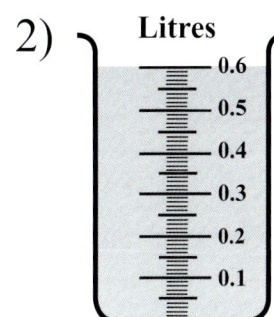 2) Litres 3) Centilitres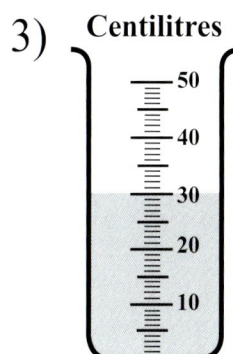

_____ ℓ   _____ ℓ   _____ cℓ

4) Millilitres   5) Millilitres 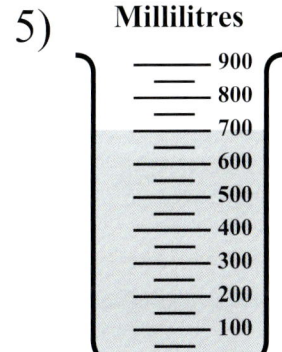   6) Centilitres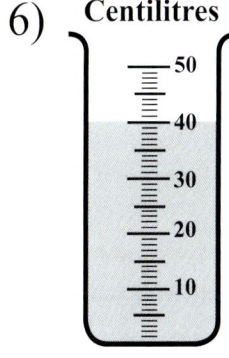
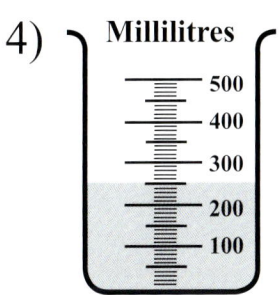

_____ mℓ   _____ mℓ   _____ cℓ

7) Litres 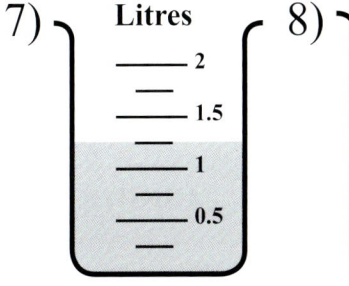   8) Millilitres 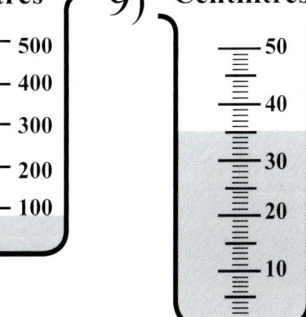   9) Centilitres   10) Centilitres

_____ ℓ   _____ mℓ   _____ cℓ   _____ cℓ

5. Greater Than or Smaller Than

When comparing the size of measurements it is best to convert everything to the smallest unit of measurement. This means mostly whole numbers are being compared.

Example: Put the correct sign (> or <) between **0.75ℓ** and **700mℓ**.

Step 1 - Using the four-step conversion method, convert **0.75ℓ** to millilitres.

0.75ℓ will become **750mℓ**.

Step 2 - Compare the size of the measurements in millilitres.

750mℓ > 700mℓ

This means **0.75ℓ** is larger than **700mℓ**.

Answer: **0.75ℓ > 700mℓ**

Exercise 10: 14

Put the correct sign (> or <) between the amounts:

1) **475cm**   0.5m
2) **560cℓ**   0.6ℓ
3) **720g**   0.75kg
4) **38mℓ**   0.4cℓ
5) **0.3km**   225m
6) **0.64ℓ**   600mℓ
7) **250kg**   0.3t
8) **800mm**   0.75m
9) **700mg**   0.9g
10) **81mm**   0.8cm

Score

48

6. Rounding Measurements

Metric measurements are often rounded to the nearest whole metric unit. For example:

2.1ℓ would be rounded to **2ℓ**.

When rounding metric measurements to a specific unit, the first decimal place is the decider, as it is when rounding decimals to whole numbers.

If the decider is between:
- **0** and **4**, the whole number stays the same.
- **5** and **9**, the whole number rounds up.

Example: Round **6.59kg** to the nearest kg.

Step 1 - The first decimal place is the decider.

In **6.59kg**, the first decimal place is **5**.

Step 2 - Round up the units from **6** to **7**.

Answer: **7kg**

Exercise 10: 15   Round the amount:

1) **7.85kg** _____ kg
2) **1.7t** _____ t
3) **7.2m** _____ m
4) **3.1cm** _____ cm
5) **5.89ℓ** _____ ℓ
6) **94mℓ** _____ cℓ
7) **993.1cm** _____ m
8) **1,275g** _____ kg
9) **526cℓ** _____ ℓ
10) **7,726kg** _____ t

7. Metric Calculations

Metric Calculations often involve metric conversions. All of the amounts must be converted to the same unit of measurement required in the answer. This must be done before any of the Four Rules of Number are applied.

Example: Add **3.82km** and **250m**, then subtract from **6km**. Give the answer in kilometres.

Step 1 - Convert all the amounts to kilometres using the four-step conversion method.
250m will become **0.25km**.

Step 2 - Do the addition using the converted amount.
3.82km + 0.25km = 4.07km

$$\begin{array}{r} 3.82 \\ 0.25 + \\ \hline 4.07 \\ {}_1 \end{array}$$

Step 3 - Subtract the result from **6km**.
6km − 4.07km = 1.93km

Answer: **1.93km**

$$\begin{array}{r} {}^5\cancel{6}.{}^9\cancel{0}{}^1\cancel{0} \\ 4.07 - \\ \hline 1.93 \end{array}$$

Exercise 10: 16   Calculate the following:

Score

1) **17.64m + 4.2m + 0.17m =** _____ m

2) **9.153ℓ − 764mℓ =** _____ ℓ

3) **42mm × 3 =** _____ cm

4) **2,000kg ÷ 2 =** _____ t

5) **5.43km + 570m + 16m** = _____km

6) **752cℓ − 163cℓ** = _____ℓ

7) **36mm × 2** = _____cm

8) **8,015m ÷ 5** = _____km

9) **3t + 1,632kg** = _____t

10) **5.18m − 39cm** = _____m and _____cm

8. Imperial Measures

Imperial Measures are a form of measurement that was in use in the United Kingdom before decimal measures were introduced in the 1970s.

It is important to be aware of Imperial units because they are still in full use in a number of countries, and some Imperial measures are still regularly used in the UK.

Weight - ounces, pounds, stones, centum weights (hundredweight) and tons.

1 pound (lb)	= **16** ounces (oz)
1 stone (st)	= **14** pounds (lbs)
1 hundredweight (cwt)	= **8** stone (st)
1 ton	= **20** hundredweight (cwt)

Length - inches, feet, yards and miles.

1 foot (ft)	= **12** inches
1 yard (yd)	= **3** feet
1 mile (m)	= **1,760** yards

Capacity - pints, quarts and gallons.

1 pint	= **20** fluid ounces
1 quart	= **2** pints
1 gallon	= **8** pints

Quantities

A dozen	= **12**
A score	= **20**

Example: How many yards are there in **half a mile**?

Step 1 - Use the conversion table to find how many yards are in a mile.
 1 mile (m) = **1,760** yards

Step 2 - Divide by **2** to find **half a mile** in yards.
 1,760 ÷ 2 = 880

Answer: **880 yards** (or **880yds**)

Exercise 10: 17 Calculate the following:

1) **2lbs** = _____ oz
2) **Half a stone** = _____ lbs
3) **4cwt** = _____ st
4) **3m** = _____ yards
5) **5 pints** = _____ fluid ounces
6) **Quarter of a ton** = _____ cwt
7) **5yd** = _____ ft
8) **Half a gallon** = _____ pints
9) **5 feet** = _____ inches
10) **6 quarts** = _____ pints

Score

9. Metric-Imperial Conversions

It is important to be aware of the following rough conversions between the metric and imperial measures.
The symbol ≈ means 'roughly equal to'.
The symbol + here means 'a little bit more than'.

Length
- 2.5cm ≈ 1 inch
- 30cm ≈ 1 foot
- 1m ≈ 1+ yards
- 1.5km ≈ 1 mile
- 8km ≈ 5 miles

Weight
- 30g ≈ 1 ounce (oz)
- 1kg ≈ 2+ pounds
- 1 metric tonne ≈ 1 imperial ton

Capacity
- 1 litre ≈ 2 pints
- 4.5 litres ≈ 1 gallon

Example: How many kilometres are there in **10** miles?

Step 1 - Use the conversion table to find roughly how many kilometres are in a mile.
8km ≈ 5 miles

Step 2 - Multiply by **2** to find **10** miles in kilometres.
$8 \times 2 = 16$

Answer: **16 kilometres** (or **16km**)

Exercise 10: 18 Estimate the following:

1) **32km** ≈ _____ miles
2) **60g** ≈ _____ oz
3) **5cm** ≈ _____ inches
4) **3 feet** ≈ _____ cm
5) **9 litres** ≈ _____ gallons
6) **10 tons** ≈ _____ tonnes
7) **3 miles** ≈ _____ km
8) **6 pints** ≈ _____ litres
9) **10 pounds** ≈ _____ kg
10) **4 yards** ≈ _____ m

10. Estimating Measurements

An **Estimation** or **Approximation** is a sensible guess or judgement. It is not based on a calculation, but on a knowledge of the rough measurement of everyday items.

The symbol ≈ means 'roughly equal to' and it is often used in estimating questions.

The following measures are useful guides for estimating:

Length

15cm ≈ The length of a pencil.

30cm ≈ An A4 piece of paper lengthways.

1m ≈ The width of a single bed or an adult pace.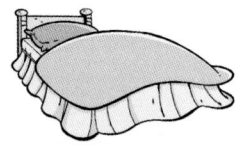

Weight

500g ≈ A can of beans.

1kg ≈ A bag of sugar.

Capacity

250ml ≈ A mug of tea.

330ml ≈ A can of drink.

1l ≈ A large carton of juice.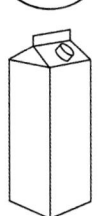

Example: What is the approximate weight of a cat?

40g   0.8kg   3kg   17kg

Step 1 - Select the closest estimation from the table that could be used to estimate the weight of a cat.
1kg ≈ A bag of sugar
A cat weighs more than a bag of sugar, so look for an amount that is more than **1kg**.

Step 2 - Rule out amounts that are too big or too small.
40g is far too light and **17kg** is much too heavy.
0.8kg is close to **1kg**, but a cat weighs more than a bag of sugar. It is likely to weigh about **3kg**.

~~**40g**~~   ~~**0.8kg**~~   **3kg**   ~~**17kg**~~
too small   too small   too big

Answer: **3kg**

Exercise 10: 19   Answer the following:

1) What is the approximate length of an A4 book?

   30cm   10cm   1.5m   90cm   50cm   _____

2) What is the approximate capacity of a tub of ice-cream?

   10ℓ   1ℓ   100mℓ   10cℓ   1cℓ   _____

3) What is the approximate weight of a bag of flour?

   5kg   1kg   500g   50g   0.75kg   _____

4) What is the approximate height of a coffee table?

   2m   50cm   10cm   10mm   20cm   _____

5) What is the approximate weight of a small dog?

   4kg   1kg   500g   50g   0.75kg   _____

6) What is the approximate capacity of a bottle of lemonade?

   5ℓ   3.5ℓ   2ℓ   100mℓ   30cℓ   _____

7) What is the approximate length of a pen?

   10cm   15cm   50cm   10mm   1m   _____

8) What is the approximate capacity of a cup of coffee?

   100mℓ   25cℓ   800mℓ   0.5ℓ   1ℓ   _____

9) What is the approximate weight of a can of peas?

   500mg   0.5kg   5kg   50g   100g   _____

10) What is the approximate width of a double bed?

   0.5m   1m   2m   70cm   80cm   _____

11. Temperature

Temperature is the measurement of how hot or cold something is. It is most commonly used to describe how hot or cold the air is in a particular place.

Temperature is measured using a thermometer in degrees Celsius (°C). A thermometer contains liquid (ethanol), which rises and falls depending on the temperature.

Water boils at **100°C** and it freezes at **0°C**.

Temperature measurements can be either **Positive** or **Negative**, in the same way as on this number line:

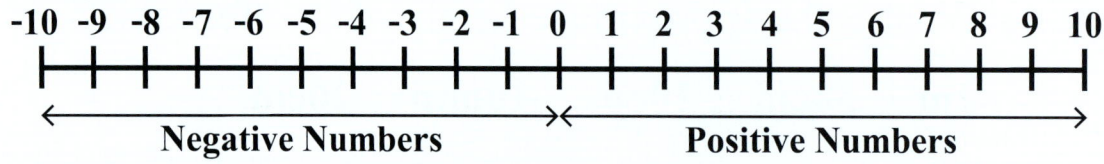

Negative numbers are used to show very cold temperatures below **0°C** (**zero**).

Example: What temperature is shown on the thermometer?

The liquid level in the thermometer rests at **-1°C** meaning that is the temperature.

Answer: **-1°C**

Exercise 10: 20

What temperature is shown on the thermometer?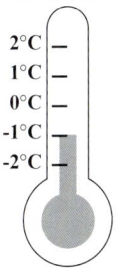

1) 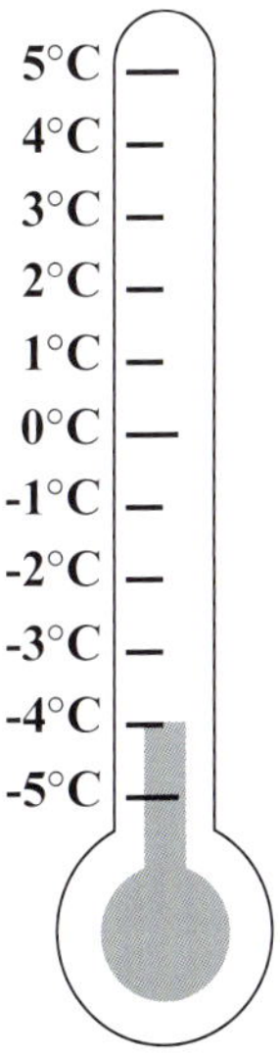 -4°C
2) 5°C
3) -2°C
4) 4°C
5) 0°C

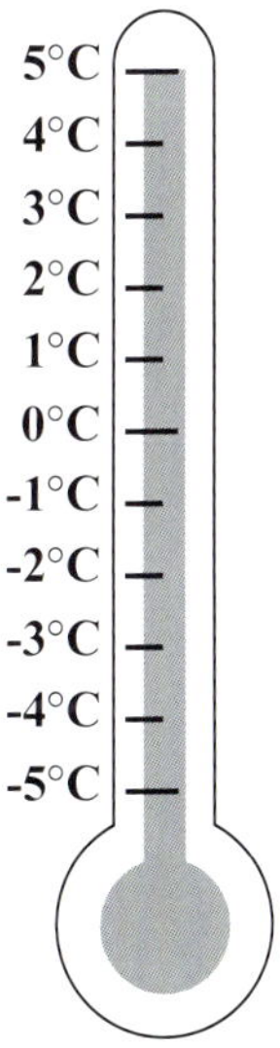

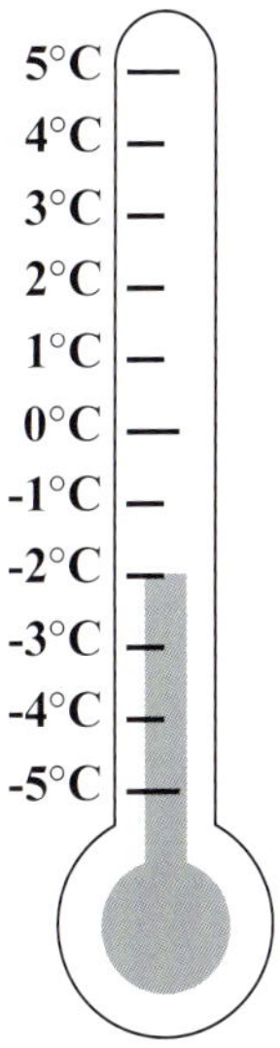

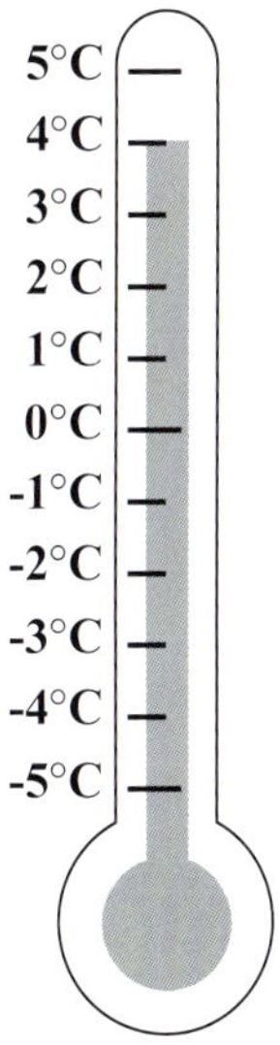

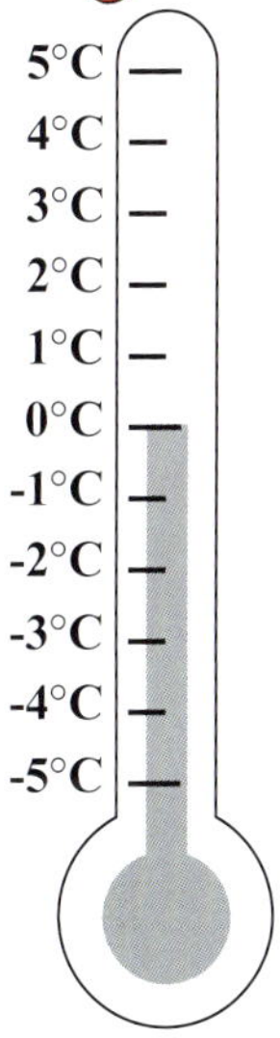

6) 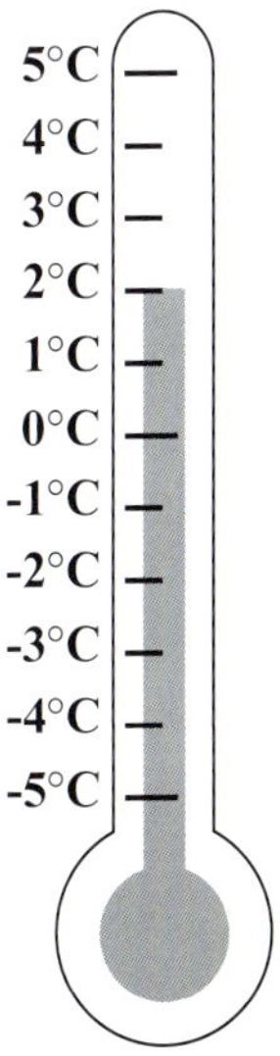 2°C
7) 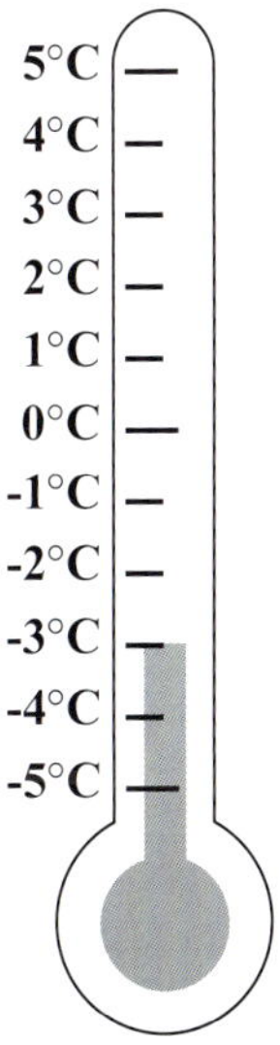 -3°C
8) 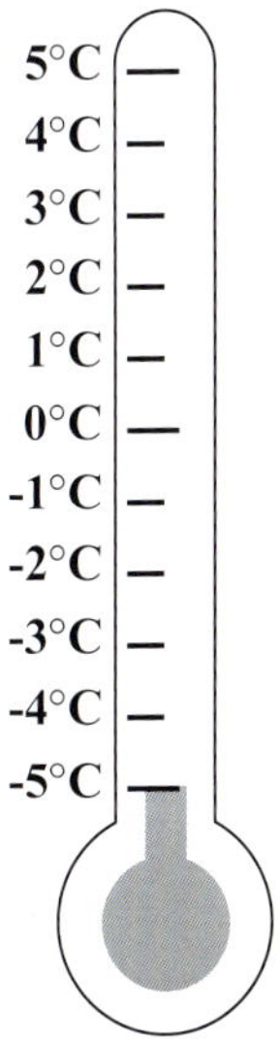 -5°C
9) 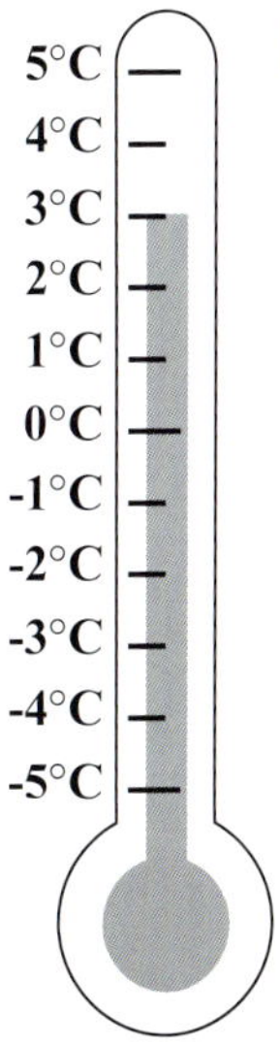 3°C
10) 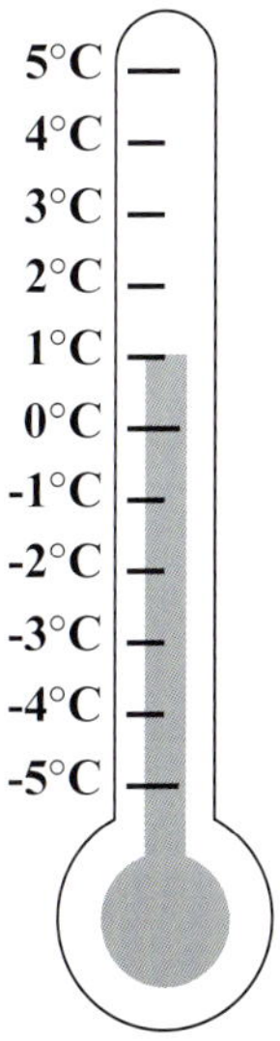 1°C

Example: What is the difference in temperature between **-2°C** and **5°C**?

Use a number line to count the gaps between **-2°C** and **5°C**.

Do not subtract one number from the other, e.g. **5 – 2 = 3**, as this is incorrect.

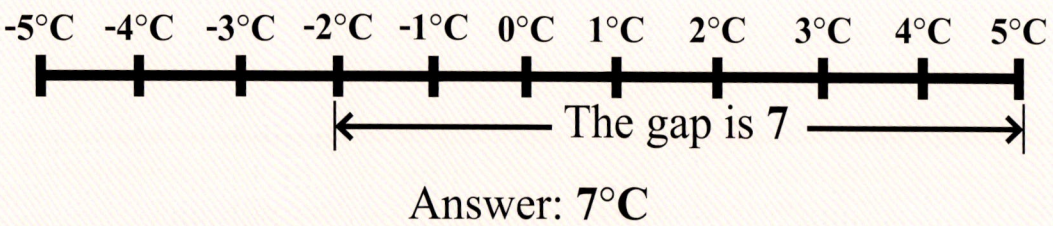

Answer: **7°C**

Exercise 10: 21 Answer the following:

1) The starting temperature was **10°C**. The temperature fell by **13°C**. What is the new temperature? ____

2) What is the difference in temperature between **-3°C** and **8°C**? ____

3) The temperature at midday was **4°C**. By nightfall the temperature had fallen by **5°C**. What was the temperature overnight? ____

4) What is the difference in temperature between **-4°C** and **5°C**? ____

5) The temperature started at **3°C**. It rose by **7°C**. What was the new temperature? ____

6) What is the difference in temperature between **0°C** and **6°C**? ____

7) The temperature in the city fell by **9°C** overnight. It started at **-1°C**. What was the new temperature? ____

8) What is the difference in temperature between **-2°C** and **-10°C**? ____

9) Overnight the temperature was **-2°C**. During the morning it rose by **8°C**. What was the new temperature? ____

10) What is the difference in temperature between **-5°C** and **7°C**? ____

Score

12. Problem Solving

Example: The total weight of Danielle, her brother and their new puppy is **81kg**. Her brother, Luca, weighs **41kg** and the puppy weighs **2,600g**. How much does Danielle weigh in kilograms?

Step 1 - Convert the weights to the unit of measurement required for the answer. This is kilograms. Using the four-step conversion method, convert the puppy's weight from grams to kilograms. **2,600g** will become **2.6kg**.

Step 2 - Add the given weights together.

41kg + 2.6kg = 43.6kg

```
  4 1 . 0
  0 2 . 6 +
  -------
  4 3 . 6
```

Step 3 - Subtract from the total amount to find Danielle's weight.

81kg – 43.6kg = 37.4kg

```
  8 1 . 0
  4 3 . 6 –
  -------
  3 7 . 4
```

Answer: **37.4kg**

Exercise 10: 22   Answer the following:

1) Shaun needs to measure **5** feet, but only has a ruler that measures in inches. How many inches does he need to measure? _____

2) Muskan is **5** feet **4** inches tall. What is her approximate height in centimetres? _____
   150cm   **160cm**   **170cm**   **140cm**   **125cm**

3) Marie needs **0.52m** of ribbon for each of **six** presents. How much ribbon does she need in total? _____

4) **1*l*** of lemonade costs **60p**. How much will **5*l*** cost? _____

5) In Italy, pizza can be purchased by the metre. Jamie orders a $\frac{3}{5}$ m long pizza and Max orders a **55cm** long pizza. Who orders the larger pizza? _____

6) A postman delivers three parcels. The first weighs **0.675kg**, the second weighs **5.1kg** and the third weighs **332g**. What is the total weight of the parcels? _____kg

7) A bridge has a weight limit of **3t and 800kg**. A lorry that weighs $3\frac{3}{4}$t needs to go over the bridge. Can the lorry cross the bridge? _____

8) If **2kg** of potatoes cost **£1.50**, how much will **4kg** cost? _____

9) Toby has made **3,000m*l*** of lemonade. He has **1*l*** bottles to put it in. How many bottles can he fill? _____

10) Yesterday, the temperature in Vancouver was **-8°C** and the temperature in New York was **2°C**. What was the difference in temperature between Vancouver and New York? _____

Chapter Eleven
AVERAGES

Data is a collection of numbers or amounts that have been grouped together for the purpose of study.

The **Average** is a general term used to describe the middle, or central, value of a group of data. There are three methods for finding this value:

Mode • **Median** • **Mean** (often called the **Average**)

Data can also be represented by the **Range**, which shows the difference between the smallest and largest amounts.

1. Mode

Mode (or Modal Value) is the number that appears most often in a set of numbers, giving a rough central value.

Example: Find the mode of these numbers:
8 1 2 6 2 7 1 2 4

Step 1 - Rearrange the numbers in size order.

1 1 2 2 2 4 6 7 8

Step 2 - Count the numbers to check all of them have been used. There are 9 numbers.

Step 3 - Select the number that appears most often. This is the mode.

1 1 2 2 2 4 6 7 8

Answer: **2**

Exercise 11: 1a Calculate the mode:

1) 60 63 57 57 16 72   Mode: _____
2) 13 12 10 13 12 13 7 8   Mode: _____
3) 2 5 7 3 4 3 7 3   Mode: _____
4) 21 25 21 24 26 29 23   Mode: _____
5) 1 3 0 10 4 1 2   Mode: _____

Score ☐

2. Median

The **Median** is the middle number in a sorted group of numbers. It gives a rough idea of the central value.

Example: Find the median of these numbers:
9 3 1 8 2 8 1 6 4

Step 1 - Rearrange the numbers in size order.
1 1 2 3 4 6 8 8 9

Step 2 - Count the numbers to check all of them have been used. There are 9 numbers.

Step 3 - Select the number that appears exactly in the middle. This is the median.

1 1 2 3 **4** 6 8 8 9

← Four numbers this side.   Four numbers this side. →

Answer: **4**

Exercise 11: 1b Calculate the median:

6) 65 64 70 80 39 19 50   Median: _____
7) 66 88 73 96 40 36 90   Median: _____

62   © 2016 Stephen Curran

8) **55 69 73 64 8 59 11**   Median: _____

9) **73 30 29 53 38 66 33**   Median: _____

10) **84 32 47 85 29 91 98**   Median: _____

3. Range

The **Range** is the distance between the smallest and the largest number in a sorted group of numbers.

Example: Find the range of these numbers:
7 5 2 6 3 2 5 8 4

Step 1 - Rearrange the numbers in size order.
2 2 3 4 5 5 6 7 8

Step 2 - Count the numbers to check all of them have been used. There are 9 numbers.

Step 3 - Subtract the smallest number from the largest number to find the range.
[2] 2 3 4 5 5 6 7 [8]
8 – 2 = 6   This is the range.

Answer: **6**

Exercise 11: 2a   Calculate the range:

Score

1) **20 24 10 34 35 21 92**   Range: _____

2) **58 54 18 84 28 53 57**   Range: _____

3) **45 63 33 66 42 43 55**   Range: _____

4) **79 66 38 43 24 92 21**   Range: _____

5) **76 92 57 77 98 41 72**   Range: _____

Exercise 11: 2b Calculate the following:

$$35 \quad 21 \quad 25 \quad 36 \quad 34 \quad 21 \quad 49$$

6) Mode: _____ 7) Median: _____ 8) Range: _____

$$57 \quad 53 \quad 54 \quad 53 \quad 55 \quad 53 \quad 57 \quad 56 \quad 58$$

9) Mode: _____ 10) Median: _____

4. The 'Mean' or Average
a. Amount to 'Mean'

The **Mean** is the **Average** of a group of numbers. It gives an accurate central value. It is calculated by adding all the amounts together and then dividing the total by the number of amounts.

Mean = Total of all the items ÷ Number of items

For example, the average of **3**, **7** and **2** is **4**.

If the calculation 3 + 7 + 2 = 12 were 'evened out' it would be 4 + 4 + 4 = 12, which gives the same answer.

Example: Find the mean of these numbers:
4 5 2 1 9 7 3 1 4

Step 1 - Add all of the numbers together to find the total.

$$4 + 5 + 2 + 1 + 9 + 7 + 3 + 1 + 4 = 36$$

Step 2 - Count how many numbers there are to find the number of items. There are **9** items.

Step 3 - Divide the total by the number of items.
$$36 \div 9 = 4$$
Answer: **4**

Exercise 11: 3   Calculate the mean:

1) 3 4 8 _____
2) 12 18 15 _____
3) 3 7 17 _____
4) 10 12 14 _____
5) 3 6 17 18 _____
6) 1 1 5 17 _____
7) 4 9 17 18 _____
8) 4 4 9 11 _____
9) 5 8 8 10 19 _____
10) 8 9 11 12 20 _____

b. 'Mean' to Total

The **Total** can be found by multiplying the mean by the number of items.
   Total of all the items = Mean × Number of items

Example: If the mean weight of **three** apples is **150g**, what is their total weight?

Step 1 - The weight of the three apples is different, but an average has already been calculated as **150g**.

Step 2 - Multiply the average by the number of apples (×**3**).
   150g × 3 = 450g
   Total = Mean × Number of items
   Answer: **450g**

Exercise 11: 4   Find the total if:

1) the average weight of **two** boxes is **887g**. _____
2) the mean height of **three** people is **165cm**. _____

3) the average cost of **five** items is **£1.64**. _____
4) the mean temperature of **four** days is **16°C**. _____
5) the average score of **nine** tests is **73**. _____
6) the mean age of **seven** children is **11**. _____
7) the average height of **six** buildings is **12m**. _____
8) the mean cost of **eight** meals is **£18.90**. _____
9) the average number of pages in **12** books is **425**. _____
10) the mean weight of **eleven** cars is **1,375kg**. _____

5. Problem Solving

Exercise 11: 5   Answer the following:

1) The total cost of **three** cakes is **£5.40**. What is the mean cost? _____

2) Anita makes hot drinks an average of **5** times a day. How many hot drinks does she make in a week? _____

James sees the following number of cars in a week:

Day	Mon	Tues	Wed	Thurs	Fri	Sat	Sun
No. of Cars	27	22	10	6	18	27	30

What is the:
3) range? _____   4) mode? _____
5) mean? _____   6) median? _____

The temperatures on one day across the world were:

City	London	Paris	Reykjavik	Dublin	Vancouver
Temperature	16°C	16°C	1°C	7°C	0°C

What was the:
7) mean? _____   8) range? _____
9) median? _____   10) mode? _____

Answers

Key Stage 2 Maths
Year 4/5 Workbook 5

Chapter Nine
Money & Costs

Exercise 9: 1
1) 910p
2) 7,105p
3) 19,506p
4) 1,058p
5) 423p
6) 250p
7) 5,871p
8) 13,694p
9) 319p
10) 742p

Exercise 9: 2
1) £3.51
2) £120.68
3) £9.30
4) £5.25
5) £38.84
6) £151.92
7) £64.17
8) £0.04
9) £6.73
10) £52.06

Exercise 9: 3
1) 0 pounds and 72 pence
2) 23 pounds and 69 pence
3) 125 pounds and 30 pence
4) 68 pounds and 99 pence
5) 104 pounds and 13 pence
6) 9 pounds and 62 pence
7) 13 pounds and 28 pence
8) 4 pounds and 56 pence
9) 55 pounds and 76 pence
10) 187 pounds and 5 pence

Exercise 9: 4
1) £103.62
2) £61.45
3) £110.17
4) £2.78
5) £29.06
6) £0.37 or 37p
7) £97.43
8) £86.52
9) £15.31
10) £100.08

Exercise 9: 5
1) £0.06 or 6p
2) £100.00 or 10,000p
3) £8.00 or 800p
4) £0.30 or 30p
5) £5.00 or 500p
6) £0.20 or 20p
7) £90.00 or 9,000p
8) £40.00 or 4,000p
9) £7.00 or 700p
10) £0.10 or 10p

Exercise 9: 6
1) £1
2) £3
3) £25
4) £5
5) £30
6) £40
7) £150
8) £100
9) £200
10) £100

Exercise 9: 7
1) £21.15
2) £17.50
3) £6.91
4) £13.08
5) £27.80
6) £18.52
7) £10.30
8) £23.03
9) £10.87
10) £54.55

Exercise 9: 8
1) £10, £2, 50p
2) £5, £2, £1, 50p, 20p, 5p, 1p
3) £20, £5, £1, 10p
4) £10, £5, £2, 20p, 5p
5) £20, 10p, 2p, 1p
6) £10, £1, 20p, 5p, 2p
7) £20, £10, £2, 50p, 10p, 2p, 1p
8) £20, £5, 50p, 20p, 10p
9) £5, £1, 5p, 2p, 1p
10) £20, £10, £5, £2, £1, 50p, 20p, 10p, 5p, 2p, 1p

Exercise 9: 9
1) £1.71
2) £3.42
3) £0.39
4) £4.27
5) £2.83
6) £4.04
7) £2.11
8) £6.22
9) £9.58
10) £3.75

Exercise 9: 10
1) 20p, 10p, 5p, 2p, 1p
2) £1, 20p, 20p, 5p, 2p
3) £2, 50p, 20p, 10p, 2p, 1p
4) £1, 10p, 5p
5) £5, 10p, 5p, 2p, 2p
6) £2, 20p, 10p, 5p, 1p
7) £10, 50p, 1p
8) £5, £2, £1, 50p, 2p, 1p
9) £20, £10, £5, £2, 50p, 5p, 1p
10) £10, £5, £1, 20p, 10p, 1p

Exercise 9: 11
1) £66.75
2) £152.83
3) £101.22
4) £135.28
5) £129.85
6) £127.84
7) £201.61
8) £86.33
9) £171.91
10) £260.49

Exercise 9: 12
1) £29.21
2) £58.62
3) £39.62
4) £80.63
5) £17.37
6) £26.78
7) £111.67
8) £81.39

Key Stage 2 Maths
Year 4/5 Workbook 5

Answers

9) £106.63
10) £83.57

Exercise 9: 13
1) £38.74
2) £219.55
3) £195.72
4) £728.76
5) £754.48
6) £238.91
7) £520.20
8) £382.90
9) £822.00
10) £810.81

Exercise 9: 14
1) 150
2) 280
3) 180
4) 220
5) 105
6) 85
7) 32
8) 50
9) 78
10) 100

Exercise 9: 15
1) £81.26
2) £2.67
3) £16.94
4) £10.26
5) £31.20
6) £5.54
7) £4.09
8) £20.44
9) £19.15
10) £20.12

Exercise 9: 16
1) £31.42
2) £3.05
3) £30.91
4) £0.49
5) £37.47
6) £19.82
7) £8.25
8) £8.12
9) £39
10) £2.01

Exercise 9: 17
1) £65.78
2) £94.20
3) £91.60
4) £9.18
5) £93.95
6) £56.14
7) £33.69
8) £65.59
9) £81.12
10) £37.90

Exercise 9: 18
1) £47.31
2) £45.53
3) £2.60
4) £97.89
5) £2.88
6) £222.85
7) £11.76
8) £126.30
9) £118.57
10) £468

Exercise 9: 19
1) £2.17
2) £19.50
3) £3.50
4) 10
5) £12.60
6) £2.50
7) £121.50
8) £0.56 or 56p

9) £107.50
10) £87.60

Chapter Ten
Measurement
Exercise 10: 1
1) 13cm
2) 2m
3) 3m
4) 2km
5) 50mm
6) 400cm
7) 5,000mm
8) 3,000m
9) 25cm
10) 6m

Exercise 10: 2
1) cm
2) km
3) cm or m
4) cm or m
5) km
6) m
7) cm
8) m
9) mm
10) mm

Exercise 10: 3
1) 2g
2) 10kg
3) 7t
4) 3kg
5) 8,000mg
6) 4,000kg
7) 5,000g
8) 6kg
9) 11g
10) 9t

Exercise 10: 4
1) kg
2) g
3) t
4) kg
5) g
6) kg
7) g
8) g
9) t
10) g

Exercise 10: 5
1) 6ℓ
2) 2ℓ
3) 3cℓ
4) 5cℓ
5) 4,000mℓ
6) 700cℓ
7) 90mℓ
8) 10ℓ
9) 8cℓ
10) 11ℓ

Exercise 10: 6
1) cℓ
2) mℓ
3) ℓ
4) cℓ or ℓ
5) mℓ or cℓ
6) ℓ
7) mℓ or cℓ
8) cℓ
9) mℓ or ℓ
10) ℓ

Exercise 10: 7
1) 2cℓ
2) 5km
3) 5kg
4) 70mm
5) 9m

Answers

Key Stage 2 Maths
Year 4/5 Workbook 5

6) 600cl
7) 8,000ml
8) 10m
9) 4t
10) 10g

Exercise 10: 8
1) 5cm and 2mm
2) 10g and 680mg
3) 4l and 300ml
4) 2m and 560mm
5) 6t and 190kg
6) 1cl and 7ml
7) 8km and 50m
8) 9l and 80cl
9) 3kg and 930g
10) 7m and 40cm

Exercise 10: 9
1) 3.037kml
2) 5.175l
3) 8.9cm
4) 7.25kg
5) 10.68m
6) 1.954g
7) 6.71l
8) 9.32t
9) 4.04m
10) 2.3cl

Exercise 10: 10
1) 0.4cm or 4mm
2) 1.3cm or 13mm
3) 2.5cm or 25mm
4) 6.8cm or 68mm
5) 3.4cm or 34mm
6) 1.7cm or 17mm
7) 3cm or 30mm
8) 3.9cm or 39mm
9) 5.2cm or 52mm
10) 2.1cm or 21mm

Exercise 10: 11
1) 0.3kg or 300g
2) 80kg or 80,000g
3) 60kg or 60,000g
4) 0.9kg or 900g
5) 75kg or 75,000g
6) 0.125kg or 125g
7) 0.55kg or 550g
8) 20kg or 20,000g
9) 0.4kg or 400g
10) 5kg or 5,000g

Exercise 10: 12
1) 250g, 50g
2) 500g, 100g, 50g
3) 250g, 50g
4) 1kg, 250g
5) 100g, 50g
6) 500g, 50g
7) 250g, 100g
8) 500g, 250g
9) 1kg, 100g, 50g
10) 100g, 50g, 10g

Exercise 10: 13
1) 0.12l
2) 0.6l
3) 30cl
4) 250ml
5) 700ml
6) 40cl
7) 1.25l
8) 80ml
9) 35cl
10) 50cl

Exercise 10: 14
1) >
2) >
3) <
4) >
5) >

6) >
7) <
8) >
9) <
10) >

Exercise 10: 15
1) 8kg
2) 2t
3) 7m
4) 3cm
5) 6l
6) 9cl
7) 10m
8) 1kg
9) 5l
10) 8t

Exercise 10: 16
1) 22.01m
2) 8.389l
3) 12.6cm
4) 1t
5) 6.016km
6) 5.89l
7) 7.2cm
8) 1.603km
9) 4.632t
10) 4m and 79cm

Exercise 10: 17
1) 32oz
2) 7lbs
3) 32st
4) 5,280 yards
5) 100 fluid ounces
6) 5cwt
7) 15ft
8) 4 pints
9) 60 inches
10) 12 pints

© 2016 Stephen Curran

Key Stage 2 Maths
Year 4/5 Workbook 5

Answers

Exercise 10: 18
1) 20 miles
2) 2oz
3) 2 inches
4) 90cm
5) 2 gallons
6) 10 tonnes
7) 4.5km
8) 3 litres
9) 5kg
10) 4m

Exercise 10: 19
1) 30cm
2) 1ℓ
3) 1kg
4) 50cm
5) 4kg
6) 2ℓ
7) 15cm
8) 25cℓ
9) 0.5kg
10) 2m

Exercise 10: 20
1) -4°C
2) 5°C
3) -2°C
4) 4°C
5) 0°C
6) 2°C
7) -3°C
8) -5°C
9) 3°C
10) 1°C

Exercise 10: 21
1) -3°C
2) 11°C
3) -1°C
4) 9°C
5) 10°C
6) 6°C
7) -10°C
8) 8°C
9) 6°C
10) 12°C

Exercise 10: 22
1) 60 inches
2) 160cm
3) 3.12m
4) £3
5) Jamie
6) 6.107kg
7) Yes
8) £3
9) 3
10) 10°C

Chapter Eleven
Averages

Exercise 11: 1a
1) 57
2) 13
3) 3
4) 21
5) 1

Exercise 11: 1b
6) 64
7) 73
8) 59
9) 38
10) 84

Exercise 11: 2a
1) 82
2) 66
3) 33
4) 71
5) 57

Exercise 11: 2b
6) 21
7) 34
8) 28
9) 53
10) 55

Exercise 11: 3
1) 5
2) 15
3) 9
4) 12
5) 11
6) 6
7) 12
8) 7
9) 10
10) 12

Exercise 11: 4
1) 1,774g
2) 495cm
3) £8.20
4) 64°C
5) 657
6) 77
7) 72m
8) £151.20
9) 5,100
10) 15,125kg

Exercise 11: 5
1) £1.80
2) 35
3) 24
4) 27
5) 20
6) 22
7) 8°C
8) 16°C
9) 7°C
10) 16°C

PROGRESS CHARTS

Shade in your score for each exercise on the graph. Add up for your total score.

9. MONEY & COSTS

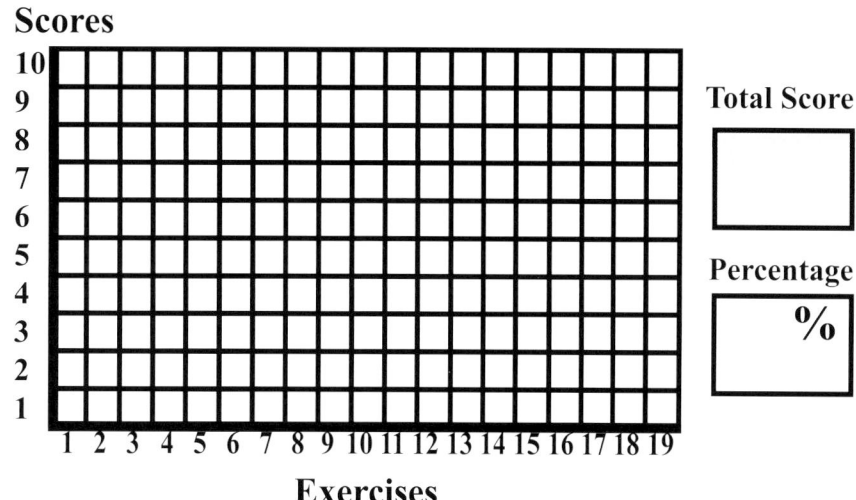

10. MEASUREMENT

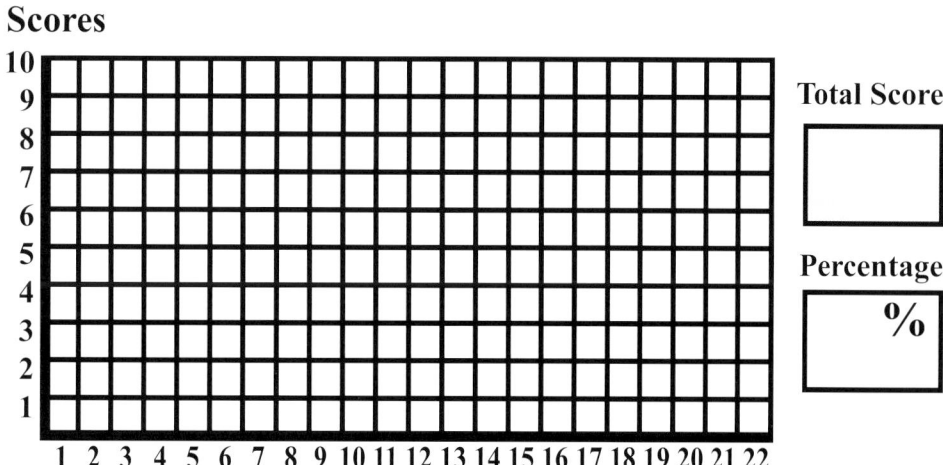

11. AVERAGES

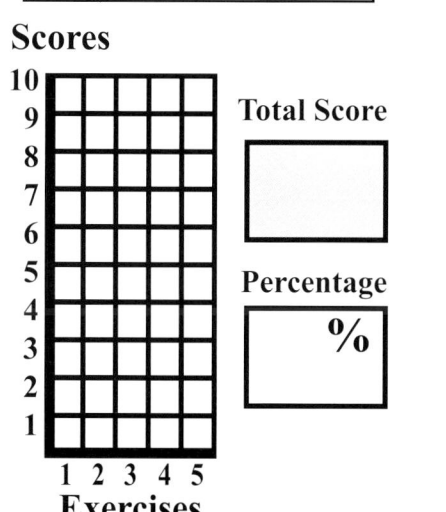

Overall Percentage %

CERTIFICATE OF ACHIEVEMENT

This certifies

_____

has successfully completed

Key Stage 2 Maths
Year 4/5
WORKBOOK 5

Overall percentage score achieved ☐ %

Comment _____

_____

Signed _____
(teacher/parent/guardian)

Date _____